PRIORITIES FOR RESEARCH TO REDUCE THE THREAT OF
FIREARM-RELATED
VIOLENCE

Committee on Priorities for a Public Health Research Agenda to Reduce
the Threat of Firearm-Related Violence

Executive Office
Institute of Medicine

Committee on Law and Justice
Division of Behavioral and Social Sciences and Education

Alan I. Leshner, Bruce M. Altevogt, Arlene F. Lee, Margaret A. McCoy,
and Patrick W. Kelley, *Editors*

INSTITUTE OF MEDICINE *AND*
NATIONAL RESEARCH COUNCIL
OF THE NATIONAL ACADEMIES

THE NATIONAL ACADEMIES PRESS
Washington, D.C.
www.nap.edu

THE NATIONAL ACADEMIES PRESS • 500 Fifth Street, NW • Washington, DC 20001

NOTICE: The project that is the subject of this report was approved by the Governing Board of the National Research Council, whose members are drawn from the councils of the National Academy of Sciences, the National Academy of Engineering, and the Institute of Medicine.

This project was supported by awards between the National Academy of Sciences and both the Centers for Disease Control and Prevention (CDC) (#200-2011-38807) and the CDC Foundation with the Foundation's support originating from The Annie E. Casey Foundation, The California Endowment, The California Wellness Foundation, The Joyce Foundation, Kaiser Permanente, the Robert Wood Johnson Foundation, and one anonymous donor. The views presented in this publication are those of the editors and attributing authors and do not necessarily reflect the view of the organizations or agencies that provided support for this project.

International Standard Book Number-13: 978-0-309-28438-7
International Standard Book Number-10: 0-309-28438-4

Additional copies of this report are available for sale from the National Academies Press, 500 Fifth Street, NW, Keck 360, Washington, DC 20001; (800) 624-6242 or (202) 334-3313; http://www.nap.edu.

For more information about the Institute of Medicine, visit the IOM home page at: **www.iom.edu.**

Printed in the United States of America

Suggested citation: IOM (Institute of Medicine) and NRC (National Research Council). 2013. *Priorities for research to reduce the threat of firearm-related violence.* Washington, DC: The National Academies Press.

THE NATIONAL ACADEMIES
Advisers to the Nation on Science, Engineering, and Medicine

The **National Academy of Sciences** is a private, nonprofit, self-perpetuating society of distinguished scholars engaged in scientific and engineering research, dedicated to the furtherance of science and technology and to their use for the general welfare. Upon the authority of the charter granted to it by the Congress in 1863, the Academy has a mandate that requires it to advise the federal government on scientific and technical matters. Dr. Ralph J. Cicerone is president of the National Academy of Sciences.

The **National Academy of Engineering** was established in 1964, under the charter of the National Academy of Sciences, as a parallel organization of outstanding engineers. It is autonomous in its administration and in the selection of its members, sharing with the National Academy of Sciences the responsibility for advising the federal government. The National Academy of Engineering also sponsors engineering programs aimed at meeting national needs, encourages education and research, and recognizes the superior achievements of engineers. Dr. C. D. Mote, Jr., is president of the National Academy of Engineering.

The **Institute of Medicine** was established in 1970 by the National Academy of Sciences to secure the services of eminent members of appropriate professions in the examination of policy matters pertaining to the health of the public. The Institute acts under the responsibility given to the National Academy of Sciences by its congressional charter to be an adviser to the federal government and, upon its own initiative, to identify issues of medical care, research, and education. Dr. Harvey V. Fineberg is president of the Institute of Medicine.

The **National Research Council** was organized by the National Academy of Sciences in 1916 to associate the broad community of science and technology with the Academy's purposes of furthering knowledge and advising the federal government. Functioning in accordance with general policies determined by the Academy, the Council has become the principal operating agency of both the National Academy of Sciences and the National Academy of Engineering in providing services to the government, the public, and the scientific and engineering communities. The Council is administered jointly by both Academies and the Institute of Medicine. Dr. Ralph J. Cicerone and Dr. C. D. Mote, Jr., are chair and vice chair, respectively, of the National Research Council.

www.national-academies.org

v

Reviewers

This report has been reviewed in draft form by individuals chosen for their diverse perspectives and technical expertise, in accordance with procedures approved by the National Research Council's Report Review Committee. The purpose of this independent review is to provide candid and critical comments that will assist the institution in making its published report as sound as possible and to ensure that the report meets institutional standards for objectivity, evidence, and responsiveness to the study charge. The review comments and draft manuscript remain confidential to protect the integrity of the deliberative process. We wish to thank the following individuals for their review of this report:

Jeremiah A. Barondess, New York Academy of Medicine
Carl C. Bell, Community Mental Health Council, Inc.
Paul Blackman, Criminal Justice Independence Institute
Charles Branas, University of Pennsylvania
John Donohue, Stanford University
Jeffrey Gunzenhauser, Los Angeles County Department of Public Health
L. Rowell Huesmann, University of Michigan
Nadine Kaslow, Emory University School of Medicine
Arthur L. Kellermann, RAND Corporation
Hyla S. Napadensky, Napadensky Energetics, Inc.
Charles H. Ramsey, Philadelphia Police Department
Robert J. Sampson, Harvard University
Donald Sebastian, New Jersey Institute of Technology

Although the reviewers listed above have provided many constructive comments and suggestions, they were not asked to endorse the conclusions or recommendations, nor did they see the final draft of the report before its release. The review of this report was overseen by **Enriqueta C. Bond,** Burroughs Wellcome Fund, and **Johanna T. Dwyer,** Tufts Medical Center. Appointed by the National Research Council and the Institute of Medicine, they were responsible for making certain that an independent examination of this report was carried out in accordance with institutional procedures and that all review comments were carefully considered. Responsibility for the final content of this report rests entirely with the editors and the institution.

Contents

Summary

Individuals use firearms legally for a variety of activities, including recreation, self-protection, and work. However, firearms can also be used to intimidate, coerce, or carry out threats of violence. Fatal and nonfatal firearm violence[1] poses a serious threat to the safety and welfare of the American public. Although violent crime rates have declined in recent years, the U.S. rate of firearm-related deaths is the highest among industrialized countries. In 2010, incidents in the United States involving firearms injured or killed more than 105,000 individuals; there were twice as many nonfatal firearm-related injuries (73,505) than deaths. Nonfatal violence often has significant physical and psychological impacts, including psychological outcomes for those in proximity to individuals who are injured or die from gun violence. The recent, highly publicized, tragic mass shootings in Newtown, Connecticut; Aurora, Colorado; Oak Creek, Wisconsin; and Tucson, Arizona, have sharpened the public's interest in protecting our children and communities from the effects of firearm violence.

In January 2013, President Obama issued 23 executive orders directing federal agencies to improve knowledge of the causes of firearm violence, the interventions that might prevent it, and strategies to minimize its public health burden. One of these executive orders noted that "in addition to being a law enforcement challenge, firearm violence is also a serious public health issue that affects thousands of individuals, families,

---

[1]For the purposes of this report, the terms "firearm violence," "gun violence," and "firearm-related violence" refer to morbidity and mortality associated with the possession and use of firearms. Firearms use a propellant or powder charge to fire a projectile and are distinct from other guns, such as BB, pellet, and other airsoft guns.

and communities across the Nation," and directed the Centers for Disease Control and Prevention (CDC), along with other relevant federal agencies, to immediately begin identifying the most pressing firearm-related violence research problems.

The CDC and the CDC Foundation[2] requested that the Institute of Medicine (IOM), in collaboration with the National Research Council (NRC), convene a committee of experts to develop a potential research agenda focusing on the public health aspects of firearm-related violence—its causes, approaches to interventions that could prevent it, and strategies to minimize its health burden. In accordance with the CDC's charge, the committee did not focus on public health surveillance and potentially related behavioral/mental health issues, as these will be addressed separately. The research program envisioned by the committee, which is designed to produce impacts in 3-5 years, focuses on

- the characteristics of firearm violence,
- risk and protective factors,
- interventions and strategies,
- gun safety technology, and
- the influence of video games and other media.

The committee identified potential research topics by conducting a survey of previous relevant research, considering input received during the workshop, and using its expert judgment. The committee was not asked to consider funding for the research agenda, and in addition to the CDC, it is likely that other agencies and private foundations will also implement the research agenda. Consequently, the committee identified a full range of high-priority topics that could be explored with significant progress made in 3-5 years. Research on these topics will improve current knowledge of the causes of firearm violence, the interventions that prevent firearm violence, and strategies to minimize the public health burden of firearm violence. To allow the research community flexibility in designing the research protocols, the report does not specify the methodologies that should be used to address the research topics.

The evidence generated by implementing a public health research agenda can enable the development of sound policies that support both

[2]The CDC Foundation's support originated from The Annie E. Casey Foundation, The California Endowment, The California Wellness Foundation, The Joyce Foundation, Kaiser Permanente, the Robert Wood Johnson Foundation, and one anonymous donor.

the rights and the responsibilities central to gun ownership in the United States. In the absence of this research, policy makers will be left to debate controversial policies without scientifically sound evidence about their potential effects.

FIREARM-RELATED VIOLENCE
AS A PUBLIC HEALTH ISSUE

The public health field focuses on problems that are associated with significant levels of morbidity and mortality. The complexity and frequency of firearm-related violence combined with its impact on the health and safety of the nation's residents make it a topic of considerable public health importance and suggest that a public health approach should be incorporated into the strategies used to prevent future harm and injuries. A public health approach involves three elements: (1) a focus on prevention, (2) a focus on scientific methodology to identify risk and patterns, and (3) multidisciplinary collaboration to address the issue. Public health strategies are designed to interrupt the connection between three essential elements: (1) the "agent" (the source of injury [weapon or perpetrator]), (2) the "host" (the injured person), and (3) the "environment" (the conditions under which the injury occurred). This public health approach has produced successes in reduction of tobacco use, unintentional poisoning, and motor vehicle fatalities.

CHARACTERISTICS OF FIREARM VIOLENCE

In order to develop relevant research questions and interventions intended to prevent firearm-related violence, it is important to understand what is and is not known about the general characteristics of both fatal and nonfatal firearm violence.

Gun type and intended use vary; so do the manifestations of firearm violence. Some firearm violence results in death, but most does not. There are important disparities across socioeconomic and ethnic groups in overall mortality rates from firearm violence. Further, there is substantial variation within each type of violence: suicide, homicide, unintentional injuries, and fatalities. For example, suicides in youth may be motivated by very different factors from those for suicides in older adults. This kind of difference will affect the success of any prevention strategy.

It is ultimately important, of course, to understand the unique characteristics of all types and subtypes of violence. However, resources focused on three specific populations—(1) the general population, (2) the general youth population, and (3) the offender population—should yield actionable information over the short term. The exact number and distribution of guns and gun types in the United States are unknown, but for each of these populations it would be valuable to have counts of total guns owned, their attributes (i.e., general type, caliber, firing mechanism), how the guns were acquired (i.e., purchased, received as a gift, traded for, stolen, etc.), and information on the sources of the guns (i.e., licensed gun dealers, friends or relatives, gun traffickers, owners of stolen guns, and so on). It also would be valuable to better understand both the violent and relevant nonviolent and self-protective behaviors of individuals with firearms.

The committee identified the following key research topics as priorities for research on characteristics of firearm violence.

- **Characterize the scope of and motivations for gun acquisition, ownership, and use, and how they are distributed across subpopulations.**
- **Characterize differences in nonfatal and fatal gun use across the United States.**

RISK AND PROTECTIVE FACTORS

The risk posed by guns is affected by a number of modifiable and unmodifiable factors, ranging from how securely guns are stored to complex society-, community-, situational-, and individual-level predictors. Society-level correlates of increased rates of firearm violence include, but are not limited to, cultural norms that support violence as an acceptable way to resolve conflicts; attitudes that regard suicide as inevitable instead of a preventable act of violence; and health, educational, economic, and social policies that maintain high levels of economic or social inequality among groups in society.

At the community level, a range of factors appears to be related to high levels of gun use. These factors include high rates of poverty, illicit drug trafficking, and substance use. For example, increased firearm violence has been associated with drug markets. A number of situational-level factors are also associated with increased risk of violence in general and firearm violence in particular. For example, the presence of drugs or alcohol increases the risk of firearm violence. Moreover, criminals often engage in violence as a means to acquire money, goods, or other rewards.

A number of individual behaviors and susceptibilities are associated with firearm violence and injury. Impulsivity, low educational attainment, substance use, and prior history of aggression and abuse are considered risk factors for violence (for both perpetrators and victims). Suicide is often associated with mental and physical health problems, financial strain, veteran status, and relationship problems. Some studies have tried to provide accurate estimates of the proportions of the general population and subpopulations with access to firearms. Less is known about the types of weapons obtained, the means of acquisition, the frequency of gun carrying in public, community-level risk and protective factors (such as the role of social norms), and degree of knowledge about and skill in firearm operation and safety, as well as how these risk and protective factors are affected by the social environment and neighborhood/community context.

The committee identified the following key research topics as priorities for research on risk and protective factors.

- **Identify factors associated with youth having access to, possessing, and carrying guns.**
- **Evaluate the potential health risks and benefits (e.g., suicide rates, personal protection) of having a firearm in the home under a variety of circumstances (including storage practices) and settings.**
- **Improve understanding of risk factors that influence the probability of firearm violence in specific high-risk physical locations.**

FIREARM VIOLENCE PREVENTION AND OTHER INTERVENTIONS

Research findings have been mixed on the effectiveness of interventions to prevent firearm violence. Successful interventions to reduce firearm-related injuries, as with many other examples in public health, must involve the health and public safety communities, educators, and other community groups. As part of a public health approach, interventions may target

- the "agent," meaning the gun or its possessor;
- the "host," or the victim(s) of firearm-related violence; and
- the "environment," including social, physical, or virtual environments that may shape gun policies, norms, and behavior.

Unauthorized gun possession or use is associated with higher rates of firearm violence than legal possession of guns. Controlling access to guns through background checks or restrictions on particular types of firearms remains controversial, and the effectiveness of various types of control is inadequately researched. Research on the impact of imposing additional penalties for firearm use in illegal activities has also produced mixed results. Studies on the impact of right-to-carry laws on firearm violence also have inconsistent results and have been debated for a decade.

Interventions Focused on Potential Perpetrators and Victims of Firearm Violence

In 2010, incidents involving firearms injured or killed more than 105,000 individuals in the United States, including approximately 19,000 suicides. Understanding differences among subpopulations with access to guns and targeting interventions to their particular risk factors may confer a public health benefit. For example, alcohol use is attributed with increased levels of firearm-related violence. However, state laws designed to ameliorate the risk of firearm use by those that abuse alcohol differ, and there is a lack of data on the basis for these laws or on their effectiveness. Risk stratification with respect to mental health and the use of firearms is imprecise and not well understood. Although the risk associated with some specific psychiatric diagnoses is better understood now than in the past, mental health issues that foster a propensity toward violence and risk taking are not well defined and not readily recognized by authorities.

Interventions Focused on Social, Physical, and Virtual Environments

It is unclear whether modifications in the physical and social environment have been effective in reducing firearm violence. Community-based programs and focused policing interventions in general have been found to be effective in reducing violence in some settings (e.g., high-risk physical locations) and appear to be more effective than prosecutorial policies, including mandatory sentences. Moreover, regulations that limit hours for on-premise alcohol sales in pubs, bars, and nightclubs have been associated with reduced violence.

Firearm safety education programs are widespread in public schools, but they are inadequately studied and the few evaluations that have been conducted provide little evidence of effectiveness. No conclusive data exist about interventions intended to reduce the number and impact of mass shootings. Additionally, although communities, schools, and campuses have developed myriad safety plans, there is very little information available about their effectiveness.

The committee identified the following key research topics as priorities for research on prevention and other interventions.

- **Improve understanding of whether interventions intended to diminish the illegal carrying of firearms reduce firearm violence.**
- **Improve understanding of whether reducing criminal access to legally purchased guns reduces firearm violence.**
- **Improve understanding of the effectiveness of actions directed at preventing access to firearms by violence-prone individuals.**
- **Determine the degree to which various childhood education or prevention programs reduce firearm violence in childhood and later in life.**
- **Do programs to alter physical environments in high-crime areas result in a decrease in firearm violence?**

IMPACT OF GUN SAFETY TECHNOLOGY

Technologies that can reduce firearm violence offer further opportunities to reduce the burden of product-related injuries. Research from the injury prevention field indicates that changing products to make them safer is frequently more effective at reducing injury and death than trying to change personal behavior. Several objectives of these gun technologies are to prevent unintentional shootings, often by very young children; the shooting of police officers by assailants using the officers' own weapons; and suicides, especially by teenagers. In addition, these prevention technologies offer the prospect of reducing firearm-related crime by rendering a gun unusable to an unauthorized person.

There are both active and passive technologies that may have an impact. Passive technologies—for example, technologies that recognize person-specific features such as voice, hand geometry, iris scans, and fingerprints—are those that confer a safety benefit without requiring any specific action by a user. Active technologies require a specific action by a user to enable the technology—for example, to activate a firearm a user has to produce an item that activates the firearm (e.g., tokens, magnetic stripe badges, or proximity cards). The development and application of these technologies to guns has been an intermittent and fragmented process complicated by the diversity in firearms themselves. Technology adoption can be facilitated or hindered by a variety of factors. To achieve a reduction of preventable deaths and injuries related to firearms, future research should examine how product safety measures are accepted and used at a population level. This includes improving understanding about factors that promote consumer adoption of gun technologies and identifying lessons learned from public health successes across states and countries.

The committee identified the following key research topics as priorities for research on gun safety technology.

- **Identify the effects of different technological approaches to reduce firearm-related injury and death.**
- **Examine past consumer experiences with accepting safety technologies to inform the development and uptake of new gun safety technologies.**
- **Explore individual state and international policy approaches to gun safety technology for applicability to the United States as a whole.**

VIDEO GAMES AND OTHER MEDIA

The vast majority of research on the effects of violence in media has focused on violence portrayed in television and the movies, although more recent research has been expanded to include music, video games, social media, and the Internet. Interest in media effects is fueled by the fact that youth are spending more time engaging with media that portrays increasing amounts of violence. Although research on the effects of media violence on real-life violence has been carried out for more than 50 years, none of this research has focused on firearm violence in particular as an outcome. As a result, a direct relationship between violence in media and real-life firearm violence has not been established and additional research is necessary.

The committee identified the following key research topic as a priority for research on video games and media.

- **Examine the relationship between exposure to media violence and real-life violence.**

RESEARCH DESIGN AND DATA

High-quality data that are usable, credible, and accessible are fundamental to both the advancement of research and the development of sound policies. Anonymous data are sufficient for these purposes, and in fact anonymized data should be used to protect civil liberties. Basic information about gun possession, distribution, ownership, acquisition, and storage is lacking. No single database captures the number, locations, and types of firearms and firearm owners in the United States. Because different forms of firearm violence respond to different strategies, without good data it is virtually impossible to answer fundamental questions about occurrence and risk factors or to effectively evaluate programs intended to reduce violence and harm. Data about the sources of guns used in crimes are important, given that studies suggest that the mechanism by which an individual acquires a gun may predict future violent use of that gun. The National Violent Death Reporting System is a beginning, but it covers only one-third of U.S. states (CDC, 2013a).

Additionally, the lack of comprehensive datasets and the wide variety of sources and the fact that the data lead to contradictory conclusions call into question the reliability and validity of gun-violence data. Technological opportunities and recent advances that can enhance linkages among datasets from other federal, state, and local sources may enable better predictive analytics, real-time information sharing, and reduction of data noise.

The predominant use of research study designs that have limited ability to study causality, like case-control and ecological studies that aggregate data from sources and levels, have compounded the challenge faced by researchers and policy makers alike. Progressing to other experimental and quasi-experimental designs that have better ability to study causality and utilizing interdisciplinary partnerships and consultations with academics, practitioners, and community members would strengthen research.

These issues related to research design and data, if not addressed, will limit the ability of researchers to perform rigorous studies, as well as the ability of policy makers to use research to inform the development and evaluation of future policies. The CDC, in collaboration with its federal and state partners, can improve the reliability and accuracy of data and research about firearm-related violence.

CONCLUSION

The research agenda proposed in this report is intended as an initial—not a conclusive or all-encompassing—set of questions critical to developing the most effective policies to reduce the occurrence and impact of firearm-related violence in the United States. No single agency or research strategy can provide all the answers. This report focuses on the public health aspects of firearm violence; the committee expects that this research agenda will be integrated with research conducted from criminal justice and other perspectives to provide a much fuller knowledge base to underpin our nation's approach to dealing with this very important set of societal issues.

Priorities for Research to Reduce the Threat of Firearm-Related Violence

INTRODUCTION

On January 16, 2013, President Barack Obama announced *Now Is the Time*, a plan to address firearm violence[1] in order "to better protect our children and our communities from tragic mass shootings like those in Newtown, Aurora, Oak Creek, and Tucson" (White House, 2013a, p. 2). These multiple-victim homicides, because of their shocking nature, have commanded the attention of the public, the media, and policy officials, even though they are relatively rare and account for a small proportion of all firearm-related injuries and deaths in the United States. Mass shootings are part of a larger, complex firearm violence burden that encompasses nonfatal and unintentional injuries, homicides, suicides, and crimes involving firearms. In the past decade, firearm-related violence has claimed the lives of more than a quarter-million people in the United States.[2] By their sheer magnitude, injuries and deaths involving firearms constitute a pressing public health problem.

Firearm-related injuries and deaths have devastating health consequences for individuals, families, and communities. In addition to these individual, familial, and community effects, public mass shootings have huge consequences for the larger society as it attempts to respond to such

---

[1] For the purposes of this report, the terms "firearm violence," "gun violence," and "firearm-related violence" refer to morbidity and mortality associated with the possession and use of firearms. Firearms use a propellant or powder charge to fire a projectile and are distinct from other guns, such as BB, pellet, and other airsoft guns.

[2] NCIPC (National Center for Injury Prevention and Control). 2013. *WISQARS injury mortality reports: Firearm deaths and rates per 100,000—2000-2010, United States, all races, both sexes, all ages* (accessed May 1, 2013).

tragedies. All these events occur in the context of a civil society that has millions of guns lawfully owned by citizens who use them for protection, hunting, sport, or work. There are also an unknown number of guns in the hands of criminals and others who are prohibited by law from possessing them.

To help minimize future firearm-related deaths, President Obama issued 23 executive orders directing federal agencies to improve knowledge of the causes of firearm violence, the interventions that prevent firearm violence, and strategies to minimize the public health burden of firearm violence (White House, 2013b). One of these executive orders, Action #14, noted that "in addition to being a law enforcement challenge, gun violence is also a serious public health issue that affects thousands of individuals, families, and communities across the Nation" (White House, 2013b). This order directed the Centers for Disease Control and Prevention (CDC), along with other relevant federal agencies, to immediately begin identifying the most pressing research problems in firearm-related violence with the greatest potential for broad public health impact. Based on this directive, the CDC and the CDC Foundation[3] requested that the Institute of Medicine (IOM), in collaboration with the National Research Council (NRC), identify questions that would define a public health research agenda for firearm violence prevention and intervention. Broadly, the committee was charged with identifying the most critical research questions in the following areas:

- The characteristics of firearm violence
- Risk and protective factors
- Interventions and strategies
- Gun safety technology
- The influence of video games and other media

The evidence generated by implementing a public health research agenda can enable the development of sound policies that support both the rights and the responsibilities central to gun ownership in the United States. In the absence of this research, policy makers will be left to debate controversial policies without scientifically sound evidence about their potential effects.

---

[3]The CDC Foundation's support originated from The Annie E. Casey Foundation, The California Endowment, The California Wellness Foundation, The Joyce Foundation, Kaiser Permanente, the Robert Wood Johnson Foundation, and one anonymous donor.

Scope of the Public Health Problem

Injuries and Fatalities

Unintentional injury is the leading cause of death in Americans aged 1 to 44 (NCHS, 2012). Firearm-related injury, in particular, is a serious threat to the health of the nation, with direct costs to the victims of violence as well as societal costs to families, friends, and communities. In 2010, there were twice as many nonfatal firearm-related injuries (73,505) as deaths.[4,5]

Between the years 2000 and 2010, firearm-related suicides significantly outnumbered homicides for all age groups, annually accounting for 61 percent of the more than 335,600 people who died from firearm-related violence in the United States.[6,7] The number of public mass shootings of the type that occurred at Sandy Hook Elementary School accounted for a very small fraction of all firearm-related deaths. Specifically, since 1983 there have been 78 events in which 4 or more individuals were killed by a single perpetrator in 1 day in the United States, resulting in 547 victims and 476 injured persons (Bjelopera et al., 2013).

Although overall crime rates have declined in the past decade and violent crimes, including homicides specifically, have declined in the past 5 years (FBI, 2011a), crime-related deaths involving firearms remain a serious threat. According to the Federal Bureau of Investigation's (FBI's) Uniform Crime Reporting Program, 68,720 people were murdered in firearm-related violence between 2007 and 2011. During that same time frame, firearms accounted for more than twice as many murders as all other weapons combined (FBI, 2011b). More than two-thirds of victims murdered by a spouse or ex-spouse died as a result of a gunshot wound (Cooper and Smith, 2011). More than 600,000 victims of

---

[4]NCIPC. 2013. *WISQARS nonfatal injury reports: Overall firearm gunshot nonfatal injuries and rates per 100,000—2010, United States, all races, both sexes, all ages* (accessed May 1, 2013).

[5]NCIPC. 2013. *WISQARS injury mortality reports: Overall firearm gunshot nonfatal injuries and rates per 100,000—2010, United States, all races, both sexes, all ages* (accessed May 1, 2013).

[6]NCIPC. 2013. *WISQARS injury mortality reports: Suicide firearm deaths and rates per 100,000—2000-2010, United States, all races, both sexes, all ages* (accessed May 1, 2013).

[7]NCIPC. 2013. *WISQARS injury mortality reports: Firearm deaths and rates per 100,000—2000-2010, United States, all races, both sexes, all ages* (accessed May 1, 2013).

robbery and other crimes reported that they faced an assailant armed with a gun (Truman and Rand, 2010).

Demographic Characteristics of Victims in the United States

There are major disparities among subpopulations of people in the United States in terms of mortality rates from firearm violence. The patterns for homicide and suicide are vastly different depending on economic conditions and geography, with homicides occurring more frequently among youth in high-poverty urban environments and suicides occurring more frequently among middle-aged males in rural areas. Inclusive of homicide, suicide, and unintentional death, African American males have the highest overall rate of firearm-related mortality: 32 per 100,000,[8] twice that of white, non-Hispanic males (at 16.6 per 100,000),[9] and three times that of Hispanic and American Indian males (at 10.4[10] and 11.8[11] per 100,000, respectively). The rate of mortality by firearm for Asian/Pacific Islander males is 4.2 per 100,000.[12] The rates of mortality for females are much lower, ranging from a low of 0.6 per 100,000 for Asian/Pacific Islander females[13] to 3.3 per 100,000 for African American and 3.0 for white, non-Hispanic females.[14] As will be discussed in further

---

[8]NCIPC. 2013. *WISQARS injury mortality reports: Overall firearm gunshot fatal injuries and rates per 100,000—2010, United States, black, males, all ages* (accessed May 15, 2013).

[9]NCIPC. 2013. *WISQARS injury mortality reports: Overall firearm gunshot fatal injuries and rates per 100,000—2010, United States, white, non-Hispanic, males, all ages* (accessed May 15, 2013).

[10]NCIPC. 2013. *WISQARS injury mortality reports: Overall firearm gunshot fatal injuries and rates per 100,000—2010, United States, Hispanic, males, all ages* (accessed April 30, 2013).

[11]NCIPC. 2013. *WISQARS injury mortality reports: Overall firearm gunshot fatal injuries and rates per 100,000—2010, United States, American Indian/Alaskan Native, males, all ages* (accessed May 15, 2013).

[12]NCIPC. 2013. *WISQARS injury mortality reports: Overall firearm gunshot fatal injuries and rates per 100,000—2010, United States, Asian/Pacific Islander, males, all ages* (accessed April 30, 2013).

[13]NCIPC. 2013. *WISQARS injury mortality reports: Overall firearm gunshot fatal injuries and rates per 100,000—2010, United States, Asian/Pacific Islander, females, all ages* (accessed April 30, 2013).

[14]NCIPC. 2013. *WISQARS injury mortality reports: Overall firearm gunshot fatal injuries and rates per 100,000—2010, United States, black, females, all ages* (accessed April 30, 2013); NCIPC. 2013. *WISQARS injury mortality reports: Overall firearm gunshot fatal injuries and rates per 100,000—2010, United States, white, non-Hispanic, females, all ages* (accessed May 15, 2013).

detail later in the report, the reasons for these differences may include a variety of factors such as socioeconomic status, urban/rural factors, and crime and policing in neighborhoods. Individual factors that may influence these differences include age; substance use; engagement or association with risky, delinquent, violent, or unlawful behaviors; propensity for suicide; and whether the perpetrator of a homicide is a family member, acquaintance, or stranger. Many of these factors are confounding, and careful analysis is required to understand the independent and interactive effects, supporting the need for rigorous research.

Availability of Firearms

Guns are widely used for recreation, self-protection, and work in the United States. However, it is difficult to determine the exact number and distribution of guns currently in homes and communities due to lack of data. Between 1986 and 2010, the domestic production of firearms increased by 79 percent, firearm exports increased by 11 percent, and firearm imports increased by 305 percent (ATF, 2012). A December 2012 poll found that 43 percent of those surveyed reported having a gun in the home (Gallup, 2013).

Defensive Use of Guns

Defensive use of guns by crime victims is a common occurrence, although the exact number remains disputed (Cook and Ludwig, 1996; Kleck, 2001a). Almost all national survey estimates indicate that defensive gun uses by victims are at least as common as offensive uses by criminals, with estimates of annual uses ranging from about 500,000 to more than 3 million (Kleck, 2001a), in the context of about 300,000 violent crimes involving firearms in 2008 (BJS, 2010). On the other hand, some scholars point to a radically lower estimate of only 108,000 annual defensive uses based on the National Crime Victimization Survey (Cook et al., 1997). The variation in these numbers remains a controversy in the field. The estimate of 3 million defensive uses per year is based on an extrapolation from a small number of responses taken from more than 19 national surveys. The former estimate of 108,000 is difficult to interpret because respondents were not asked specifically about defensive gun use.

A different issue is whether defensive uses of guns, however numerous or rare they may be, are effective in preventing injury to the gun-wielding crime victim. Studies that directly assessed the effect of actual defensive uses of guns (i.e., incidents in which a gun was "used" by the crime victim in the sense of attacking or threatening an offender) have found consistently lower injury rates among gun-using crime victims compared with victims who used other self-protective strategies (Kleck, 1988; Kleck and DeLone, 1993; Southwick, 2000; Tark and Kleck, 2004). Effectiveness of defensive tactics, however, is likely to vary across types of victims, types of offenders, and circumstances of the crime, so further research is needed both to explore these contingencies and to confirm or discount earlier findings.

Even when defensive use of guns is effective in averting death or injury for the gun user in cases of crime, it is still possible that keeping a gun in the home or carrying a gun in public—concealed or open carry—may have a different net effect on the rate of injury. For example, if gun ownership raises the risk of suicide, homicide, or the use of weapons by those who invade the homes of gun owners, this could cancel or outweigh the beneficial effects of defensive gun use (Kellermann et al., 1992, 1993, 1995). Although some early studies were published that relate to this issue, they were not conclusive, and this is a sufficiently important question that it merits additional, careful exploration.

Firearm-Related Violence as a Public Health Issue

The public health field focuses on problems that are associated with significant levels of morbidity and mortality. The complexity and frequency of firearm-related violence combined with its impact on the health and safety of the nation's residents make it a topic of considerable public health importance and suggest that a public health approach should be incorporated into the strategies used to prevent future harm and injuries. Violence, including firearm-related violence, has been shown to be contagious. Recognizing this, the academic community has suggested that research examine violence much like is done for contagious diseases (IOM, 2013).

In the past, responses to firearm violence typically have been based in the criminal justice system, which is crucial to public safety, but a more comprehensive and multidisciplinary approach is necessary to reduce the burden of firearm-related violence on individuals, families, communities, and general society (Kellermann et al., 1991). Public health approaches focus efforts on the prevention of violence by characterizing the scope or magnitude of the problem, evaluating potential risk and protective factors associated with specific outcomes, and developing and evaluating interventions to affect these risk factors (Satcher, 1995).

Topics previously viewed as purely criminal in nature, such as firearm-related violence, require a multidisciplinary approach (Kellermann et al., 1991) because, frequently, health and crime share the same risk and protective factors, or complex determinants (Akers and Lanier, 2009; Akers et al., 2013). Public health and behavioral and social science (to include criminology) are two compatible disciplines that together can aid understanding and address broad challenges to health and safety, as both disciplines benefit from scientific methods and from each other's perspectives. A recent example of this synergism is reflected in a bulletin by the Department of Justice devoted to the application of public health principles to violent crime (Markovic, 2012).

Developing an integrated and collaborative public health and criminal justice injury prevention paradigm will improve interventions to reduce harms associated with firearm-related violence. This approach was suggested in the 1985 *Surgeon General's Workshop on Violence and Public Health* (HHS and DOJ, 1996) and in a 1985 NRC and IOM report *Injury in America: A Continuing Public Health Problem*. This recommended strategy has been reaffirmed and reinforced over the years, including in a 1999 IOM report *Reducing the Burden of Injury: Advancing Prevention and Treatment*, which argued that "the injury field has much to contribute to scientific understanding of firearm injuries and to the prevention of violence, complementing the contributions made by criminal justice, mental health, and other approaches" (p. ix).

Applying Public Health Strategies to Reducing Firearm Violence

A public health approach involves three elements: (1) a focus on prevention, (2) a focus on scientific methodology to identify risk and patterns, and (3) multidisciplinary collaboration to address the issue (IOM, 2008). The ecological framework, a tool used in both criminology and public health, may further guide the analysis of potential interventions to achieve the necessary scale to prevent or reduce firearm violence. The sheer number of firearm-related injuries and fatalities, coupled with the broad range of settings and circumstances under which firearm violence can occur, requires a multidimensional approach based on the interrelation among individual characteristics, family history and dynamics, community context and gun availability, and national or international influences. This multidimensional approach is necessary in order to direct an intervention at the level of influence necessary to bring about the desired change.

Assessing and ultimately implementing public health strategies to deal with societal problems requires a comprehensive research agenda with contributions from the many scientific disciplines relevant to understanding the complex etiology and prevention of firearm violence (Hemenway and Miller, 2013). For example, public health outcomes research may include an investigation of product safety options combined with strategies to change the "prevalence, social norms, and cultures of harmful behaviors" (Mozaffarian et al., 2013, p. 551; see also Hemenway, 2001; Mozaffarian et al., 2012).

Beginning in the late 1960s, a comprehensive approach was adopted based largely on the work of William Haddon, who developed a model for the systematic exploration of causation and countermeasures based on the epidemiological triangle of host, agent, and environment in the pre-event, event, and post-event phases (Haddon, 1967, 1968, 1980). Such strategies are designed to interrupt the connection among three essential elements: (1) the "agent" (the source of injury [weapon or perpetrator]), (2) the "host" (the injured person), and (3) the "environment" (the conditions under which the injury occurred). This public health approach has produced successes in reduction of tobacco use, unintentional poisoning, and motor vehicle fatalities. These successes suggest the following strategies for reducing firearm-related injuries:

- Individual- and family-level interventions focused on the victim (host) pre-event:
  o Routine primary care counseling
  o Education
  o Family risk factors
- Individual-, family-, or community-level interventions focused on the perpetrator or gun (agent) pre- or post-event:
  o Recognition of at-risk behaviors
  o Early detection of risk factors
  o Safety standards
  o Active protection (requires an overt action by the user)
  o Passive protection (requires no action by the user)
- Community- and society-level interventions focused on the environment pre- or post-event:

- o   Hotlines
- o   Licensing
- o   Public education and media campaigns
- o   Economic development (to decrease concentrated disadvantage)
- o   Physical environment (e.g., converting vacant lots to green spaces)

Motor vehicle–related injury reduction provides a useful analogy for using a public health approach to a problem that also has criminal justice considerations. For example, in both motor vehicle and gun use, there is a need to balance health and safety with the practical reality of a potentially dangerous tool that is embedded in U.S. society.

Efforts to reduce motor vehicle–related injuries were limited initially to improving driver skills (licensing in the 1930s) and evolved to include safety technology (collapsible steering columns, shatter-resistant glass, and seat belts in the 1950s and 1960s). This approach resulted in a multifaceted effort based on

- thorough data analysis and surveillance systems—tracking trends and patterns in injuries and identifying research questions;
- performance standards—setting safety standards for vehicles;
- research in behavioral human factors and engineering—examining the host, agent, and environment (injury mechanisms, crashworthiness, vehicle safety countermeasures, road characteristics);
- state and local programs addressing equipment and human factors such as fatigue and alcohol; and
- public education and law enforcement programs.

A similar multifaceted program, through the development of a public health research agenda, is needed to ultimately reduce the burden of gun violence.

Study Goals, Methods, and Organization of the Report

Study Process and Methods

The committee was charged with articulating the topics that should make up a public health firearm violence research agenda (see Box 1). The charge to the committee included conducting an expert assessment of critical research questions, developing guidance, and recommending priorities for the CDC within a 3-month time frame. To meet this obligation the committee held a single 4-day meeting on April 22-25, 2013. The meeting included a public workshop and closed sessions of the committee for deliberations and report drafting (see Appendix B for the open agenda). The workshop was organized in order to hear from a range of authorities in the area of firearm violence research; policy makers and advocates with long-standing interest in gun policy; and researchers with expertise in injury prevention, media influences, and firearms technology, as well as to seek general public comment about the development of a public health research agenda to reduce firearm-related violence.

In addition, the committee performed a literature review on the specific research areas to be addressed. The committee also considered the data and research methodology challenges in the area of firearm-related violence. The committee identified potential research topics by conducting a survey of previous relevant research, considering input received during the workshop, and using its expert judgment. The committee was not asked to consider funding for the research agenda, and in addition to the CDC, it is likely that other agencies and private foundations will also implement the research agenda. Consequently, the committee identified a full range of high-priority topics that could be explored with significant progress made in 3-5 years. Research on these topics will improve current knowledge of the causes of firearm violence, the interventions that prevent firearm violence, and strategies to minimize the public health burden of firearm violence. To allow the research community flexibility in designing the research protocols, the report does not specify the methodologies that should be used to address the research topics. However, the committee does provide examples of specific questions that could be explored under each research topic.

BOX 1
Statement of Task

An ad hoc committee will be appointed to develop for the Centers for Disease Control and Prevention a proposed public health research agenda to improve knowledge of the causes of gun violence, the interventions that prevent gun violence, and strategies to minimize the public health burden of gun violence. Consideration of optimal methodological approaches to address gaps in knowledge is also important.

The proposed agenda should identify the most critical research questions that can be answered in the short term (particularly within a 3-year time frame). In the view of the committee, the answers to the questions should be those with the potential for the greatest public health impact and shed light on the characteristics of gun violence and the potential to prevent gun violence. As general guidance on the extent of the envisioned research program, the proposed agenda should be one that could be completed in 3-5 years:

- **Characteristics of gun violence:** Identify research questions necessary to improve understanding of the characteristics of both fatal and non-fatal gun violence.
- **Interventions and strategies:** Identify research questions that are necessary to improve understanding of the effectiveness of interventions and strategies to prevent or reduce gun-related injuries. These may include, but should not be limited to, research questions related to the impact of public education campaigns, youth access to and use of guns, safe storage practices, access to guns, and improved personal protection.
- **Technology:** Identify research questions related to the impact of potential technologies that may reduce gun-related violence, including how guns and ammunition can be designed and engineered to improve safety and prevent misuse.
- **Video games and other media:** Identify questions that improve the understanding and impact of violence in video games, the media, and social media on real-life violence.
- **Risk and protective factors:** Identify research questions that will assess potential risk and protective factors and other critical issues, such as the socioeconomic and socio-cultural environment.

With respect to the scope of the recommended research agenda, the areas of public health surveillance and behavioral/mental health should not be a focus of the committee's work. Additionally, questions related to clinical practice and treatment should not be a focus. The committee will produce a brief consensus report that may include a summary of the most significant research gaps, a consolidation of committee findings, and the identification of proposed research questions to inform the public health approach to preventing gun violence.

Organization of the Report

The section that follows discusses issues related to research design and data and their impact on being able to undertake a public health research agenda. Subsequent sections discuss sequentially each of the five specific research areas the committee was charged with examining

1. characteristics of firearm violence,
2. risk and protective factors,
3. interventions and strategies,
4. gun technology, and
5. influence of video games and other media.

Each section includes an abbreviated summary of background, past and ongoing research, major issues and controversies, and the challenges going forward. Following the overview of each of these research domains, the committee identifies the topics that should constitute a public health research agenda to reduce and prevent firearm-related injuries and fatalities.

AN OVERARCHING ISSUE: RESEARCH DESIGN AND DATA

Throughout its deliberations, the committee identified a series of issues related to data and research methods that would impact the design and implementation of its proposed research agenda. These issues related to research design and data, if not addressed, will limit the ability of researchers to perform rigorous studies as well as limit the ability of policy makers to use research to inform the development and evaluation of future policies.

The CDC, by working with its federal and state partners, can improve the reliability and accuracy of data and research about firearm-related violence. An interagency approach is necessary because the data currently used in research on firearm violence come largely from datasets developed for other purposes, such as crime and health research, and cover topics that are broader than firearm violence. Technological opportunities and recent advances that can enhance linkages among datasets from other federal, state, and local sources may enable better predictive analytics, real-time information sharing, and reduction of nonessential data and inconsistencies and thereby improve the quality of firearm-related research.

Impact of Existing Federal Restrictions on Firearm Violence Research

There are many legal and responsible uses for guns; an individual's right to own and possess guns was established in the U.S. Constitution and affirmed in the 2008 and 2010 Supreme Court rulings in *District of Columbia v. Heller*[15] and *McDonald v. City of Chicago*.[16] However, the scarcity of research on firearm-related violence limits policy makers' ability to propose evidence-based policies that reduce injuries and deaths and maximize safety while recognizing Second Amendment rights. Since the 1960s, a number of state and federal laws and regulations have been enacted that restrict government's ability to collect and share information about gun sales, ownership, and possession, which has limited data collection and collation relevant to firearm violence prevention research. Among these are the amendments to the Gun Control Act of 1968,[17] which prohibits the federal government from establishing an electronic database of the names of gun purchasers and requires gun dealers to conduct annual inventories of their firearms.

In addition to the restrictions on certain kinds of data collection, congressional action in 1996 effectively halted all firearm-related injury research at the CDC by prohibiting the use of federal funding "to advocate or promote gun control."[18] In 2011, Congress enacted similar restrictions affecting the entire U.S. Department of Health and Human Services.[19] The net result was an overall reduction in firearm violence research (Kellermann and Rivara, 2013). As a result, the past 20 years have witnessed diminished progress in understanding the causes and effects of firearm violence.

---

[15]554 U.S. 570 (2008).

[16]561 U.S. 3025 (2010).

[17]Public Law 90-618, 82 Stat. 1213 (October 22, 1968).

[18]Omnibus Consolidated Appropriations Act, 1997, Public Law 104-208, 104th Cong., 110 Stat. 3009, p. 244 (September 30, 1996).

[19]Consolidated Appropriations Act 2012, Public Law 112-74, 112th Cong., 125 Stat. 786, Sec. 218, p. 1085 (December 23, 2011).

Data Quality, Accessibility, and Aggregation

High-quality data that are usable, credible, and accessible are fundamental to both the advancement of research and the development and evaluation of sound policies. Policy makers need a wide array of information, including community-level data and data concerning the circumstances of firearm deaths, types of weapons used, victim–offender relationships, role of substance use, and geographic location of injury—none of which is consistently available. The absence of these kinds of appropriate baseline data make it difficult to answer fundamental questions about prevalence, determine etiology, or effectively evaluate programs for potential reduction of harm and injury. Given civil liberty concerns, it will be important that all data used in research be anonymized.

Some data related to firearm violence may not reflect the full scope of the problem. Firearm violence research is based on statistically uncommon events, which would require very large sample sizes to measure effects in small geographic units of analysis. Consequently, researchers often rely on aggregated (at the national or state level) or proxy measures of gun ownership and violence (NRC, 2005). The result is a lack of individual-level data that could reveal more useful information about local trends and causes of firearm violence.

Data to Assess Gun Acquisition and Storage

Basic information about gun possession, acquisition, and storage is lacking. No single database captures the total number, locations, and types of firearms and firearm owners in the United States (NRC, 2005). Data about the sources of guns used in crimes are important because the means of acquisition may reveal opportunities for prevention of firearm-related violence. Currently, such information is collected predominantly by the Bureau of Alcohol, Tobacco, Firearms and Explosives (ATF), which traces weapons submitted by police agencies. The ATF tracks firearm possession and subsequent use only after a gun is used in a crime. Even if the ATF is able to successfully trace a firearm from its original point of purchase, the firearm may have changed hands many times without a paper trail (both legally and illegally) after its original purchase. As a result, the sources identified when guns are traced by the ATF are unrepresentative of the proximate sources of guns used in crimes, and ATF data may exaggerate the share of guns that have attributes associated with gun trafficking, such as quick movement from first retail sale to recovery by police in connection with a crime (Kleck and Wang, 2009). Improving the representativeness of ATF tracing data might help researchers better understand the link between gun sources and gun crime.

Data Fragmentation and Standardization

Existing data are housed in a number of discrete databases (NRC, 2005; Zawitz, 1995), which contributes to data limitation and fragmentation. One attempt to remedy the fragmentation is the CDC's National Violent Death Reporting System (NVDRS). The system provides information about firearm deaths in the context of all violent deaths, including child abuse, intimate partner homicide, and suicide, but is limited to only 18 U.S. states (CDC, 2013a). Some localities, but not all, use the Weapon Related Injury Surveillance System (WRISS), which is a surveillance system that standardizes the collection of data on individuals treated for gunshot wounds and assaults in emergency departments (Massachusetts Executive Office of Health and Human Services, 2013). However, although there is a need, none of the existing databases, alone or combined, provide "comprehensive, timely, and accurate data needed to answer many important questions pertaining to the role of firearms in violent events," as was called for in a 2005 NRC report (p. 48).

The lack of standardization across databases limits their comparability (NRC, 2005). The absence of clearly defined concepts complicates data collection and interpretation. For example, definitions of "self-defense" and "deterrence" are ambiguous (NRC, 2005; Weiner et al., 2007). There is no standardized method for data collection or collation, which prevents researchers from harnessing the potential power of data across multiple datasets.

Research Methods and Challenges

Research on firearm violence that addresses the causal chain for tying a cause to an effect will provide important insights. This is especially true regarding research on gun availability and homicide. The widespread use of research study designs that have limited ability to study causality, like case-control and ecological studies, which aggregate data from sources and levels, poses challenges for interpretation among both researchers and policy makers. Moving forward it will be important to utilize other experimental and quasi-experimental designs that have better ability to study causality, including, for example, longitudinal studies. Firearm-related research would be strengthened through interdisciplinary partnerships and consultations among academics, practitioners, and community members. Research activities should be designed to ensure that findings will help to illuminate and estimate the prevalence and distribution of risk and protective factors and aid in evaluation of programs. There are important testable questions regarding adoption, fidelity, adaptation, sustainability, and scale-up of programs that necessitate collaboration between researchers and the practitioners who will use the findings to inform implementation strategies.

CHARACTERISTICS OF FIREARM VIOLENCE

Fatal and nonfatal firearm violence poses a serious threat to the safety and welfare of the American public. As discussed in the Introduction, there are legal and responsible uses for firearms, including law enforcement, self-defense, and recreational uses. However, the presence of guns in civil society can also lead to firearm-related violence. Although violent crime rates have declined in recent years (Truman, 2011), the U.S. rate of firearm-related homicide is higher than that of any other industrialized country: 19.5 times higher than the rates in other high-income countries (Richardson and Hemenway, 2011). In 2010, incidents involving firearms injured or killed more than 105,000 individuals in the United States.[20] A recent estimate suggested that firearm violence cost the United States more than $174 billion in 2010 (Miller, 2010). However, it is essentially impossible to quantify the overall physiological, mental, emotional, social, and collateral economic effects of firearm violence, because these effects extend well beyond the victim to the surrounding community and society at large (IOM, 2012).

Very little is understood about the exact scope and nature of firearm violence in the United States, including the distribution of guns. The cir-

---

[20]NCIPC. 2013. *WISQARS injury mortality reports: Overall firearm gunshot nonfatal injuries and rates per 100,000—2010, United States, all races, both sexes, all ages* (accessed April 30, 2013); NCIPC. 2013. *WISQARS injury mortality reports: 2010, United States, firearm deaths and rates per 100,000—all races, both sexes, all ages* (accessed April 30, 2013).

cumstances under which firearm violence occurs vary widely. Mortality rates associated with firearm violence differ based on the shooter's intent, the type of firearm used, and the specific nature of the injury (Beaman et al., 2000).

In order to develop relevant research questions and targeted interventions to prevent firearm-related violence, it is important to understand what is and is not known about the general characteristics of both fatal and nonfatal firearm violence.

Types and Numbers of Firearms

No one knows exactly how many guns exist in the United States. In 2007, one estimate placed the total number of firearms in the country at 294 million: "106 million handguns, 105 million rifles, and 83 million shotguns" (Krouse, 2012, p. 8). Based on this estimate, the United States has the most guns per capita of any nation in the world[21] (Karp, 2007). U.S. gun owners typically own more than one gun (Cook and Ludwig, 1996; Hepburn et al., 2007).

In general, there are three characteristics that define individual guns: gun type, firing action, and ammunition. "Gun type" distinguishes guns by external physical characteristics; for instance, "handguns" are designed to be gripped with one hand and "long guns" are designed to be fired from the shoulder. In 2004, handguns made up approximately 40 percent of all firearms owned in the United States (Hepburn et al., 2007). For both handguns and long guns, the firing action ranges from manual to semiautomatic to automatic, reflecting the mechanism by which successive shots are fired. Guns with manual firing actions are capable of one shot at a time with a delay for manual loading of the individual bullets; semiautomatic guns can fire shots in rapid sequence but require individual trigger pulls for each shot; and automatic guns can reload and fire many bullets with a single pull of the trigger, delayed only by the automatic ejection of the spent casing and loading of a fresh cartridge. Finally, different guns use different ammunition. The "caliber" of a gun refers to the internal diameter of the bore of the weapon. The "gauge" of a shotgun refers to the number of bore-fitting balls that equal 1 pound.

Gun preference typically depends on the gun's intended use. For example, hunters typically use long guns. Surveys of felons found a prefer-

---

[21]Averaging 88.8 guns per 100 people. Serbia has the second greatest number of guns per capita, averaging 59 guns per 100 people.

ence for larger-caliber handguns that are easily concealable (Sheley and Wright, 1995; Wright and Rossi, 1986). Handguns are used in more than 87 percent of violent crimes (BJS, 2010).

Types of Firearm Violence

At the broadest level, firearm violence is either fatal or nonfatal. Within the category of fatal incidents, types of violence include suicides, homicides, and unintentional fatalities. Mass shootings may be considered either a separate category or a subset of homicides. Those types of firearm violence vary substantially with respect to the typical shooter, intent, and population affected. Similarly, there is substantial variation among the types of nonfatal violence, which encompass unintentional and intentional injuries, threats, and defensive use of guns. Thus, it is important to understand the distinctive characteristics of the various types and subtypes of violence. For example, suicides in youth may be motivated by very different factors from those in older adults, a divergence that will affect the design of any prevention strategy. However, suicides and homicides share a very important characteristic that is important here, namely, that most acts appear to be reactive and unplanned.

Suicide

Firearm-related suicides—though receiving far less public attention— significantly outnumber homicides for all age groups, with suicides accounting for approximately 60 percent of all firearm injury fatalities in the United States in 2009 (Kochanek et al., 2011). In 2010, suicide was the 10th leading cause of death among individuals in the United States over the age of 10 (CDC, 2012a). Although the U.S. population's age-adjusted, firearm-related suicide rate had been generally declining since 1999, it slowly began to rise again after 2006.[22] Rural areas tend to have higher rates of firearm suicides than urban areas, while urban areas have higher rates of firearm homicides (Branas et al., 2004). However, differences in suicide

---

[22]NCIPC. 2013. *WISQARS injury mortality reports: 1999-2010, United States, suicide firearm deaths and rates per 100,000—all races, both sexes, all ages, output by year, age-adjusted* (accessed April 30, 2013).

rates in urban versus rural areas may also be related to socioeconomic differences among those areas.[23]

The public health burden of suicide varies by subpopulation. Males are more likely than females to die by suicide, and firearms are the most common method of suicide for males (CDC, 2012a). Between 2005 and 2010, firearm suicide rates were greatest for whites, followed by blacks, American Indians/Alaskan Natives, and Asians/Pacific Islanders.[24] Moreover, certain age groups are associated with higher suicide rates. In 2009, suicide was the third leading cause of death for American youth between the ages of 15 and 19 (Heron, 2012), but overall firearm suicide rates were highest for individuals over the age of 75 between 2005 and 2010.[25] In contrast to urban areas, rural areas tend to have lower rates of firearm homicide and higher rates of firearm suicide; this urban-rural disparity is, however, not evident for non-firearm suicide (Branas et al., 2004; Hirsch, 2006; Singh and Siahpush, 2002).

In 2010, firearms were used in the majority of the 38,364 suicide deaths in the United States (Hoyert and Xu, 2012). A wide array of other lethal measures, such as hanging, suffocation, and jumping from heights, are available for suicide. For example, between 2005 and 2009, for every 100 suicide attempts in which a firearm was used, more than 83 ended in death, but the fatality rate for suffocation was similar, at almost 80 per 100 (CDC, 2013b). Because firearms are only one lethal method for committing suicide, it is not clear how public health initiatives to reduce firearm-related suicides will affect the total public health burden of suicide. Further, it is not understood how frequently firearms are associated with premeditated or impulsive suicides. Therefore, additional data about context of suicides are required to develop and evaluate interventions that are designed to reduce the burden of firearm-related suicides and suicides in general.

---

[23]NCHS (National Center for Health Statistics). 2013. *Underlying cause of death, 1999-2010, intentional self-harm, African American, grouped by urbanization.* http://wonder.cdc.gov (accessed May 15, 2013). Data from CDC WONDER online database, released 2012. Data are from the Multiple Cause of Death Files, 1999-2010, as compiled from data provided by the 57 vital statistics jurisdictions through the Vital Statistics Cooperative Program.

[24]NCIPC. 2013. *WISQARS injury mortality reports: 2005-2010, United States, suicide firearm deaths and rates per 100,000—all races, both sexes, all ages, output by race, age-adjusted* (accessed April 30, 2013).

[25]NCIPC. 2013. *WISQARS injury mortality reports: 2005-2010, United States, suicide firearm deaths and rates per 100,000—all races, both sexes, ages 0 to 85+, output by age-group* (accessed May 15, 2013).

Homicide

According to the FBI's Uniform Crime Report, 46,313 people were murdered in incidents involving firearms between 2007 and 2011 (FBI, 2011b). During that same time, firearms accounted for more than twice as many murders as all other weapons combined (FBI, 2011b). Approximately 3 percent of firearm-related assaults known to the police (which represent a portion of total firearm-related assaults) are fatal (computed from FBI, 2011c).

The risk of homicide by firearm is not distributed equally across the U.S. population. Individuals living in urban areas experience higher rates of firearm-related homicides than individuals in rural areas (Branas et al., 2004). Both victims and perpetrators of firearm-related homicides tend to be male (Cooper and Smith, 2011). In the vast majority of murders for which the victim–offender relationship is known, the victim is a member of the same race as the offender and is acquainted with the offender (Cooper and Smith, 2011). Homicides by a stranger, friend, or acquaintance are more likely to involve a gun than those committed by an intimate partner or family member (Cooper and Smith, 2011). An important subset of fatal firearm-related incidents involves domestic violence. A study by Sorenson (2006) found that guns are used more often than other types of weapons when females are the victims of intimate partner homicide.

The risk of homicide by firearm varies by race and ethnicity. In 2010, the firearm-related homicide rate was significantly higher for blacks than Asian/Pacific Islanders, whites, and American Indian/Alaskan Natives.[26] Studies have shown that racial differences in socioeconomic status, residential segregation, or neighborhood environmental hazards account for some or all of the overall racial differences in homicide (Greenberg and Schneider, 1994; Howard et al., 2000; Onwuachi-Saunders and Hawkins, 1993). Additionally, younger populations represent a large proportion of homicide victims and perpetrators (Cooper and Smith, 2011).

Handguns account for the vast majority of firearm-related homicides; in 2011, "handguns comprised 72.5 percent of the firearms used in murder and non-negligent manslaughter incidents" (FBI, 2011b, p. 2). On the other hand, rifles and shotguns are less frequently used to commit homicides (U.S. Census Bureau, 2012), although they are more lethal than handguns (Kleck, 1984).

---

[26]NCIPC. 2012. *WISQARS injury mortality reports: 2010, United States, homicide firearm deaths and rates per 100,000—all races, both sexes, all ages, grouped by race, age-adjusted* (accessed April 30, 2013).

Unintentional Fatalities

Unintentional firearm-related deaths have steadily declined during the past century.[27] The number of unintentional deaths due to firearm-related incidents accounted for less than 1 percent of all unintentional fatalities in 2010 (Hoyert and Xu, 2012). Despite this progress, more than 600 people in the United States died as a result of an unintentional discharge of a firearm in 2010 (Hoyert and Xu, 2012). Risks are highest among adolescents and young adults. Approximately 10 percent of unintentional deaths in 2010 involved children under age 15 (Hoyert and Xu, 2012).

About half of unintentional firearm-related fatalities are self-inflicted (Hemenway et al., 2010). Unintentional firearm-related deaths caused by someone other than the victim are primarily committed by friends or family members (Hemenway et al., 2010). Only 2 percent of unintentional firearm-related deaths were connected with self-defense (Hemenway et al., 2010). Rates of unintentional firearm death are significantly higher in rural than in urban counties (Carr et al., 2012).

Mass Shootings

According to the Congressional Research Service, public mass shootings "have claimed 547 lives and led to an additional 476 injured victims" since 1983 (Bjelopera et al., 2013, pp. 7-8). Mass shootings are a highly visible and moving tragedy, but represent only a small fraction of total firearm-related violence. Although it may seem that protection against such an event is nearly impossible, proactive law enforcement activities, including community policing and intelligence-led policing, may help prevent some mass shootings (Bjelopera et al., 2013). Analyzing the details of a prevented event against those of a realized event might provide guidance to schools and other locations with large groups of people about efficient and effective ways to avoid such an event. Proactive mental health risk assessment and interventions may also prevent some mass shootings. It is also apparent that some mass murder incidents are associated with suicides (Bell and McBride, 2010). However,

---

[27]The CDC's WISQARS (Web-based Injury Statistics Query and Reporting System) website cautions against comparing the number of deaths and death rates from 1998 and earlier with data from 1999 and later due to significant changes in mortality data coding (CDC, 2011a).

the characteristics of suicides associated with mass murders are not understood.

Nonfatal Firearm Violence

Homicides, suicides, and accidental deaths do not capture the full impact of firearm violence. In 2010, nonfatal firearm violence, including intentional and unintentional injuries, affected almost 24 out of every 100,000 individuals,[28] including 15,576 children and adolescents under the age of 20.[29] Individuals seen in hospitals for unintentional firearm injuries are usually male (Sinauer et al., 1996). As with suicides, rural areas tend to have higher rates of firearm-related unintentional injuries than urban areas (Nance et al., 2002). Most suicide attempts involving a gun end in death; few nonfatal gunshot injuries result from this cause.

Guns also can be used to intimidate and coerce through threats of violence. In 2010, firearms were involved in less than 6 percent of the total 3,148,250 reported aggravated or simple assaults (Truman, 2011). Similarly, less than 7 percent of all rapes or sexual assaults in 2010 involved a firearm (Truman, 2011).

Sources of Guns

To address the criminal misuse of firearms leading to death or injury, it is important to understand how "firearms move from lawful commerce into the hands of criminals" (ATF, 2011, p. i). A survey of gun owners between 2005 and 2010 found that an average of 232,400 guns were stolen each year (Langton, 2012). Although research in the 1980s suggested that criminals acquired guns primarily through theft (Wright and Rossi, 1986), more recent prisoner surveys suggest that stolen guns account for only a small percentage of guns used by convicted criminals (Harlow, 2001; Zawitz, 1995). It is, however, unclear whether prisoners are willing to admit to gun thefts in government-conducted surveys. According to a 1997 survey of inmates, approximately 70 percent of the guns used or possessed by criminals at the time of their arrest came from family or friends,

---

[28]NCIPC. 2012. *WISQARS injury mortality reports: Overall firearm gunshot nonfatal injuries and rates per 100,000—2010, United States, all races, both sexes, all ages, age-adjusted* (accessed April 30, 2013).

[29]NCIPC. 2012. *WISQARS injury mortality reports: Overall firearm gunshot nonfatal injuries and rates per 100,000—2010, United States, all races, both sexes, 0-19, age-adjusted* (accessed April 30, 2013).

drug dealers, street purchases, or the underground market (Harlow, 2001). Another 14 percent of those surveyed bought or traded guns at retail stores, pawnshops, flea markets, or gun shows (Harlow, 2001). However, some experts question the validity of commonly used research methodologies for identifying crime-gun-trafficking prevalence, arguing that trafficking is more closely associated with gun scarcity than inappropriate acquisition from licensed gun dealers (Kleck and Wang, 2009). A better understanding of the validity of different methods to evaluate the sources of crime guns would help inform policies aimed at disrupting the flow of guns to criminals.

Research Questions

There is a pressing need to obtain up-to-date, accurate information about how many guns are owned in the United States, their distribution and types, how people acquire them, and how they are used. Policies that seek to reduce the health burden of firearm-related violence can be strengthened by being grounded in sound information about the possession of guns for nonviolent as well as violent purposes. This kind of information should be obtained for three broad populations of interest: (1) the general population of the United States, (2) the youth population of the United States, and (3) offenders. To help achieve a better understanding of the characteristics of gun violence, the following two research topics were identified as priorities.

Characterize the scope of and motivations for gun acquisition, ownership, and use, and how are they distributed across subpopulations.

Examples of information that could be examined:

- Collect data about gun ownership, acquisition, and use for various groups within the U.S. general population.
  - Focus on those at greatest risk of causing injury.
  - Focus on those at greatest risk of injury—urban and rural youth, racial/ethnic minority populations, and those living in concentrated poverty.

- Collect data about the sources (e.g., gifts, purchases), means (e.g., theft, trafficking), and legality of possession by various groups, particularly offenders.

Characterize differences in nonfatal and fatal gun use across the United States.

Examples of topics that could be examined:

- What are the characteristics of non-self-inflicted fatal and nonfatal gun injury?
  - What attributes of guns, ammunition, gun users, and other circumstances affect whether a gunshot injury will be fatal or nonfatal?
  - What characteristics differentiate mass shootings that were prevented from those that were carried out?
  - What role do firearms play in illicit drug markets?
- What are the characteristics of self-inflicted fatal and nonfatal gun injury?
  - What factors (e.g., storage practices, time of acquisition) affect the decision to use a firearm to inflict self-harm?
  - To what degree can or would prospective suicidal users of firearms substitute other methods of suicide?
- What factors drive trends in firearm-related violence within subpopulations?
- What factors could bring about a decrease in unintentional firearm-related deaths?

RISK AND PROTECTIVE FACTORS ASSOCIATED WITH FIREARM-RELATED VIOLENCE

Trends in firearm-related injury and death differ by type of violence. Between 2005 and 2010, the percentage of firearm-related violent victimizations remained generally stable (Truman, 2011). As stated above, overall firearm-related suicide rates generally declined between 1999 and

2006, but then began to climb.[30] Additionally, firearm-related death rates for youth ages 15-19 declined from 1994 to 2009 (Dowd and Sege, 2012). The reasons for the decline in firearm-related youth violence are unclear, although some experts credit improving socioeconomic conditions, general violence prevention programs, a declining crack/cocaine market, and increased community policing (Dowd and Sege, 2012).

It is important to understand how certain factors can affect the risk of different types of violence. As set forth below, a number of modifiable and unmodifiable factors affect the risks posed by possession and use of guns, including factors as straightforward as how guns are stored and as complex as society-, community-, situational-, and individual-level predictors.

Society-Level Factors

At the societal level, income inequality emerges as a powerful predictor of firearm homicide and violent crime. Research suggests that income inequality undermines social cohesion and social capital, which in turn, increases firearm violence (Kennedy et al., 1998). Other studies have shown that high-income countries with high levels of firearm availability also have higher rates of female homicide, after controlling for income inequality (Hemenway et al., 2002). Research on international variation in homicides also shows a link with income inequality possibly mediated by low levels of trust, a proxy for social capital (Elgar and Aitken, 2011). Poor mental health, chronic environmental and social stressors, racial and income inequalities, gender inequalities, high rates of unemployment, and a lack of educational and employment opportunities are all associated with higher rates of firearm violence (WHO, 2002).

Violence prevention programs, legislative reforms, and declines in firearm availability may contribute to decreased firearm violence (Dowd and Sege, 2012). Some studies identify an association between increased firearm legislation (including firearm purchase background checks) (Sumner et al., 2008) and lower rates of fatal firearm violence (Fleegler et al., 2013), while other studies have not found this correlation (Hahn et al., 2005).

---

[30]NCIPC. 2013. *WISQARS injury mortality reports: 1999-2010, United States, suicide firearm deaths and rates per 100,000—all races, both sexes, all ages, output by year, age-adjusted* (accessed April 30, 2013).

Community-Level Factors

At the community level, a range of factors appears to be related to high levels of violence, consistent with the previously introduced concept of the contagion of violence. These include high rates of residential mobility, social isolation, unemployment, and illicit drug trafficking. For example, increased firearm violence has been associated with drug markets (Blumstein and Cork, 1996; Goldstein, 1985; Kennedy et al., 1996). This prevalence could be a consequence of drug dealers carrying guns for self-defense against thieves or other adversaries who are likely to be armed. Furthermore, in communities with street drug markets, especially those where such markets are ubiquitous, individuals not involved in the drug markets have similar incentives for possessing guns (Blumstein, 1995; Blumstein and Cork, 1996).

With regard to exposure to violence, "the burden of neighborhood risk falls unambiguously on minorities" (Zimmerman and Messner, 2013, p. 441), contributing to observed racial and ethnic disparities. These disparities, however, are largely accounted for by family/individual factors (lower levels of household socioeconomic status, higher rates of violent peer exposure and previous violent behavior) and neighborhood risk factors (high levels of concentrated disadvantage, deficiency of youth services) (Zimmerman and Messner, 2013). Additionally, low collective efficacy (defined as "social cohesion among neighbors combined with their willingness to intervene on behalf of the common good" [Sampson et al., 1997, p. 918]), is negatively associated with perceived violence, victimization, and homicide (Sampson et al., 1997). In turn, "concentrated disadvantage, immigrant concentration, and residential instability explain most of the variation" (Sampson et al., 1997, p. 922) (70 percent) in measures of collective efficacy. Much of the racial variation (more than 60 percent) in perpetration of violence "is explained by immigration status, marriage, length of residence, verbal/reading ability, impulsivity, and neighborhood context" (Sampson et al., 2005, p. 231), with neighborhood context being the most important (Sampson et al., 2005). Diminished economic opportunities, high concentrations of impoverished residents, high levels of transiency, high levels of family disruption, low levels of community participation, and socially disorganized neighborhoods are risk factors for youth violence overall.

Situational Factors

A number of situational factors are also associated with increased firearm violence. The presence of, or use of, drugs or alcohol is associated with assaultive and firearm violence (Garbarino et al., 2002; Nielsen and Martinez, 2003; Scribner et al., 1995; Shepherd et al., 2006). Moreover, criminals often engage in violence as a means to acquire money, goods, or other rewards; however, many instances of violence often are impulsive, angry responses to perceived or experienced social or physical threats (Connor et al., 2003). Some social and psychological research suggests that the need to defend social status may increase the likelihood and severity of response to provocation in the presence of an audience (Griffiths et al., 2011; Papachristos, 2009). Strong evidence also exists that observing a gun can "prime" aggressive behavior in certain situations, especially among those prone to aggression (Anderson et al., 1998; Berkowitz and LePage, 1967). Drinking to excess, drug use, recreational pursuit of fun (Jensen and Brownfield, 1986), involvement in drug dealing or group drug use (Sparks, 1982), gang membership (Jensen and Brownfield, 1986), involvement in minor or violent offending (Sampson and Lauritsen, 1990), and other lifestyle factors increase the risk of victimization. Other studies have delineated the finding that there is often significant overlap between victims and offenders in that they may share a set of routine activities (Osgood et al., 1996) or lifestyles (Hindelang et al., 1978) or have high levels of aggression or low self-control (Jennings et al., 2010), or that offenders may victimize one another because they believe they can do so with impunity from law enforcement (Sparks, 1982). Other situational factors, such as excessive heat (Anderson et al., 1995) or the presence of community disorder (or "broken windows") (Wilson and Kelling, 1982), have been cited as contributors to violence, although research is conflicting (Anderson et al., 1995; Butke and Sheridan, 2010).

Specific locations may also be more closely tied to certain types of firearm-related violence. Based on 2008 data from the NVDRS, almost half of firearm homicides occurred in a house, apartment, or surrounding property; one-quarter occurred on public streets or highways; and natural areas, vehicles, parking lots, parks or athletic areas, hotels/motels, and commercial areas accounted for most of the remaining murder scenes (Karch et al., 2011).

Individual-Level Factors

Individual behaviors and susceptibilities are associated with firearm violence and injury. In general, "impulsivity, low educational attainment, substance use, and prior history of aggression and abuse are considered" (WHO, 2002, p. 13) risk factors for violence, for both victims and perpetrators. Substance use, especially alcohol use, and isolation are risk factors for firearm violence (WHO, 2002). Suicide is associated with living alone, substance use, depressive symptoms (Kung et al., 2003), unemployment (Reeves et al., 2012), recent military active duty status (Gibbons et al., 2012), acute crises, and relationship problems (Kaplan et al., 2009).

Certain behaviors and characteristics associated with adolescence are also positively correlated with increased risk for firearm violence. Youth firearm ownership is associated with antisocial behavior (such as bullying, theft, vandalism, violence, substance abuse, and school misbehavior) (Cunningham et al., 2000). Studies have shown that weapon carrying among youth is closely related to having been victimized or having witnessed violence and having high levels of aggression (Fitzpatrick, 1997; Webster et al., 1993). There is also evidence that youth who carry guns may do so because they feel vulnerable to victimization (Simon et al., 1997), although other studies have found gun carrying to be a component of highly aggressive delinquency (Webster et al., 1993).

Risk factors for unintentional firearm-related fatalities include carelessness; reckless activities (e.g., playing with guns); ignorance ("I didn't know the gun was loaded"); a prior history of traffic citations, drunk driving, and arrests (Kleck, 1991); and alcohol and drug use (Ruddell and Mays, 2004). Research on victims of penetrating injury has found 5-year reinjury rates as high as 44 percent, with a 20 percent overall mortality rate (Sims et al., 1989). In addition, the risk of future gun carrying (Champion and DuRant, 2001; Spano et al., 2012) and future violence is associated with exposure to violence in general (Ehrensaft et al., 2003; Finkelhor et al., 2009; Spano et al., 2010) and firearm-related violence in particular (Bingenheimer et al., 2005; Slovak and Singer, 2001). Indirect exposure to violence, such as living in a particularly violent neighborhood, is also associated with individual behavioral health risk factors for violence, including anxiety, depression, and posttraumatic stress disorder (PTSD), which can lead to interpersonal or self-inflicted gun violence (Buka et al., 2001; Sharkey et al., 2012).

Conversely, various "direct protective" and "buffering protective" factors may minimize the effects of certain risk factors (Hall et al., 2012, p. S3). For example, high grade point average; religiousness; consistent, close, respectful relationships with parents; and involvement in social activities are protective factors against violence among youth (CDC, 2011b).

Research Questions

Three important research topics were identified by the committee: (1) factors associated with youth having access to, possessing, and carrying guns; (2) the impact of gun storage techniques on suicide and unintentional injury; and (3) "high-risk" geographic/physical locations for firearm violence.

Factors Associated with Youth Having Access to, Possessing, and Carrying Guns

In 2010, firearms accounted for 84 percent of youth (ages 10-19) homicides, and guns are the most frequent suicide method (39 percent).[31] In 2011, the Youth Behavioral Risk Survey revealed that almost 17 percent of high school students had carried a firearm, knife, or club in the past 30 days. More than 5 percent had carried a gun. The same survey showed that 15.8 percent of high school students surveyed had seriously considered attempting suicide in the previous year, and 7.8 percent had actually made a suicide attempt (CDC, 2012b).

Among rural youth, firearm ownership levels are high. Studies among rural youth reveal that about half of students in some rural communities own guns, with almost 80 percent of rural males reporting gun ownership and often multiple gun ownership (58 percent) (Slovak and Carlson, 2004). Other studies have associated youth exposure to violence

---

[31]NCIPC. 2013. *WISQARS injury mortality reports: Homicide injury deaths and rates per 100,000—2010, United States, all races, both sexes, ages 10 to 19* (accessed May 8, 2013); NCIPC. 2013. *WISQARS injury mortality reports: Homicide firearm deaths and rates per 100,000—2010, United States, all races, both sexes, ages 10 to 19* (accessed May 8, 2013); NCIPC. 2013. *WISQARS injury mortality reports: Suicide injury deaths and rates per 100,000—2010, United States, all races, both sexes, ages 10 to 19* (accessed May 8, 2013); NCIPC. 2013. *WISQARS injury mortality reports: Suicide firearm deaths and rates per 100,000—2010, United States, all races, both sexes, ages 10 to 19* (accessed May 8, 2013).

with higher levels of anger, dissociation, PTSD, higher levels of violent behaviors, and lower levels of parental monitoring (Buka et al., 2001; Fowler et al., 2009; Slovak and Singer, 2001; Zona and Milan, 2011).

Methods that may be used to investigate these questions include ethnographic and qualitative research strategies, survey methods (including the Youth Behavioral Risk Survey), and community-based participatory approaches.

Identify factors associated with juveniles and youths having access to, possessing, and carrying guns.

Examples of topics that could be examined:

- Which individual and/or situational factors influence the illegal acquisition, carrying, and use of guns by juveniles?
- What types of weapons do youths obtain and carry?
- How do youths acquire these weapons (e.g., through legal or illegal means)?
- What are key community-level risk and protective factors (such as the role of social norms), and how are these risk and protective factors affected by the social environment and neighborhood/community context?
- What are key differences between urban and rural youth with regard to risk and protective factors for firearm-related violence?

Impact of Having a Firearm at Home

A recent Pew Foundation report found that "the vast majority of gun owners say that having a gun makes them feel safer. And far more today than in 1999 cite protection—rather than hunting or other activities as the major reason for why they own guns" (Pew Research Center, 2013). Despite gun owners' increased perception of safety, research by Kellermann et al. (1992, 1993, 1995) describes higher rates of suicide, homicide, and the use of weapons involved in home invasion in the homes of gun owners. However, other studies conclude that gun ownership protects against serious injury when guns are used defensively (Kleck and Gertz, 1995; Tark and Kleck, 2004).

Additional research is needed to weigh the competing risks and protective benefits that may accompany gun ownership in different communities. This information will be invaluable to individuals wanting to make an informed decision about the benefits and risks of keeping a gun in their home versus other self-protection strategies such as with nongun weapons, stalling/reasoning/arguing tactics, or calling police. The possibility for increased risk of harm in some fraction of homes will be important to understand in designing effective harm mitigation strategies, such as the use of lockboxes or gun safes for weapon storage (Grossman et al., 2005; Johnson et al., 2006).

Evaluate the potential health risks and benefits (e.g., suicide rates, personal protection) of having a firearm in the home under a variety of circumstances (including storage practices) and settings.

Examples of topics that could be examined:

- What are the associated probabilities of thwarting a crime versus committing suicide or sustaining an injury while in possession of a firearm?
- What factors affect this risk/benefit relationship of gun ownership and storage techniques?
  - o What is the impact of gun storage methods on the incidence of gun violence—unintentional and intentional—involving both youths and adults?
  - o What is the impact of gun storage techniques on rates of suicide and unintentional injury?

Public Health Approaches to Firearm Violence Focused on Particular Types of Locations

Public health approaches to ameliorating gun violence have built upon models from other public health successes, such as tobacco control and automobile safety. These successful models have used population-based approaches such as taxation, public education, efforts to change social norms, and engineering safety. But violence, and firearm-related violence in particular, is not evenly distributed in the population. Violence may concentrate geographically (Cusimano et al., 2010; Sparks, 2011), including in areas of "concentrated disadvantage," where a collection of social and economic indicators correlate strongly with a wide variety of indicators of poor health outcomes (Ross and Mirowsky, 2001). Although violence can lead to direct health outcomes—e.g., homicides and suicides—exposure to violence can also affect other health outcomes (Wilson et al., 2004; Wright and Steinbach, 2001; Ylikoski, 1995), possibly mediated by stress and a reduced sense of safety that inhibits preventive or health-seeking behaviors.

Criminologists and law enforcement officials have identified "hotspots," or high-risk physical locations, for violent crime. A number of police and criminal justice programs, such as Operation CeaseFire, Cure Violence, Project Exile, and Project Safe Streets, have attempted to reduce gun-related violence in those neighborhoods. In addition, efforts to improve the physical environment through "greening" of vacant lots have led to a decrease in gun crime, vandalism, stress, and physical inactivity in urban neighborhoods (Branas et al., 2011).

Although rates of homicide are monitored, the impact of such programs on other forms of violence and other health outcomes receives less attention (Wilson et al., 2004). While these hotspot locations tend to be located in areas of concentrated disadvantage, not all such areas have high rates of violence-related outcomes. Research is needed to better characterize these hotspot areas by the range and levels of risk—across geographic space, temporal space, situations, and relationships—and health-related outcomes including, but not limited to, violence.

A research agenda should examine communities that show positive health-related outcomes and identify modifiable risk factors that may impact both gun-related violence and other associated health risks at the neighborhood or sub-neighborhood levels. Such factors may include policing and criminal justice programs as well as other inherent social and physical environments or health services features that can be affected through programs and policies. Methodological approaches that may be used to address these questions include geospatial and social network analyses and ethnographic research.

Improve understanding of risk factors that influence the probability of firearm violence in specific high-risk physical locations.

Examples of topics that could be examined:

- What are the characteristics of high- and low-risk physical locations?
- Are the locations stable or do they change?
- What factors in the physical and social environment characterize neighborhoods or sub-neighborhoods with higher or lower levels of gun violence?

- Which characteristics strengthen the resilience of specific community locations?
- What is the effect of stress and trauma on community violence, especially firearm-related violence?
- What is the effect of concentrated disadvantage on community violence, especially firearm-related violence?

FIREARM VIOLENCE PREVENTION AND OTHER INTERVENTIONS

Successful interventions to reduce firearm-related injuries, like many other public health efforts, must involve the health and public safety communities, educators, and other community groups. During the past 20 years, significant declines in death and injury from automobile crashes, fires, and drowning have been achieved through comprehensive prevention strategies that recognize the characteristics of the agent, the victim, and the physical and social environment in which the injury occurred. A similar public health framework may be particularly effective in the case of gun violence (Hemenway, 2001; Hemenway and Miller, 2013) if the interactions of these characteristics are analyzed.

Prevention strategies may affect one or all of these players through a systems or holistic approach, and they can be applied at the time and location of imminent risk (e.g., removing guns temporarily when suicide risk is high), at times of transition (e.g., under an order of protection for domestic violence), or prior to periods of high risk (e.g., interventions for young children).

For more than two decades, research findings on the effectiveness of interventions to prevent firearm violence have been mixed. Gun possession is associated with violence, but direct causation is difficult to establish. A paucity of reliable and valid data, as discussed in the sections above, is a major barrier to the development of the most effective policies, strategies, and interventions for prevention of firearm violence. Nonetheless, many interventions have been developed and studied, and they point to areas requiring important additional research.

Targeting Unauthorized Gun Possession or Use

Reducing Unauthorized Access

Whether gun restrictions reduce firearm-related violence is an unresolved issue. One recent study found that the states with the most firearm legislation have a smaller number of firearm fatalities (Fleegler et al., 2013). It is not clear whether this legislation is affecting firearm violence directly or whether states where there is less firearm violence tend to pass more laws related to guns. Analysis of unintentional gun fatalities in 50 states revealed positive associations between the number of guns and the number of fatalities (Miller et al., 2001). Other studies found that gun restrictions had no net impact on major violence and crime (Kleck and Patterson, 1993).

Background checks are intended to curtail gun sales to prohibited persons, such as felons, the severely mentally ill, domestic violence perpetrators, and minors. But prohibited individuals may obtain firearms without background checks through unlicensed sellers at gun shows and private sales or through straw purchases.[32] Most felons report obtaining the majority of their firearms from informal sources (NRC, 2005).

There is empirical evidence that gun turn-in programs are ineffective, as noted in the 2005 NRC study *Firearms and Violence: A Critical Review.* For example, in 2009, an estimated 310 million guns were available to civilians in the United States (Krouse, 2012), but gun buy-back programs typically recover less than 1,000 guns (NRC, 2005). On the local level, buy-backs may increase awareness of firearm violence. However, in Milwaukee, Wisconsin, for example, guns recovered in the buy-back were not the same guns as those most often used in homicides and suicides (Kuhn et al., 2002).

Prosecutorial Interventions

Research on the impact of issuing sentences with additional penalties for using a firearm in the commission of a crime has revealed mixed results (McDowall et al., 1992). Most studies found that enhanced sentencing did not affect crime rates (Marvell and Moody, 1995). Other studies found decreases in some types of crimes (Abrams, 2012; NRC, 2005). In Boston, where both mandatory sentences for illegal carrying and enhanced sentenc-

---

[32]A "straw purchase" occurs when the buyer of a firearm would not pass required background checks or does not want his or her name associated with the purchase of the firearm and therefore uses someone else to make the actual purchase.

ing for use of firearms were in place at the same time, it was difficult to attribute impact to any particular policy (NRC, 2005).

Research results on the impact of right-to-carry laws on firearm violence are also inconsistent and have been debated for a decade. The 2005 NRC study found no persuasive evidence from available studies that right-to-carry laws decreases or increases violent crime.

"Gun courts," which are set up specifically to try firearm-related crimes, have not been studied adequately (NRC, 2005). In Birmingham, Alabama, gun courts have sped up the trial process, involved parental education, provided boot camp for youth, and given judges authority to impose consequences. Gun courts have been established in Brooklyn and Queens, New York; Cambridge, Massachusetts; Philadelphia, Pennsylvania; and Providence, Rhode Island.

Individual Risk and Protective Factors

Protective Effects of Gun Ownership

Estimates of gun use for self-defense vary widely, in part due to definitional differences for self-defensive gun use; different data sources; and questions about accuracy of data, particularly when self-reported. The NCVS has estimated 60,000 to 120,000 defensive uses of guns per year. On the basis of data from 1992 and 1994, the NCVS found 116,000 incidents (McDowall et al., 1998). Another body of research estimated annual gun use for self-defense to be much higher, up to 2.5 million incidents, suggesting that self-defense can be an important crime deterrent (Kleck and Gertz, 1995). Some studies on the association between self-defensive gun use and injury or loss to the victim have found less loss and injury when a firearm is used (Kleck, 2001b).

Risk Factors Associated with Gun Possession

Certain aspects of suicide, homicide, and unintentional injury may be amenable to public health research. Some studies have concluded that persons who keep a firearm in the home may have a greater risk of suicide and homicide (Kellermann et al., 1993). Homicide by individuals possessing guns illegally is of special interest. The public health burden of interpersonal firearm violence and the interactions of substance use, abuse, and trafficking deserve specific attention.

Two-thirds of homicides of ex- and current spouses were committed with firearms (Fox and Zawitz, 2007). In locations where individuals under restraining orders to stay away from current or ex-partners are prohibited from access to firearms, female partner homicide is reduced by 7 percent (Vigdor and Mercy, 2006). Research on restricted access to firearms in 46 large U.S. cities from 1979 to 2003 indicated that restricted access was associated with reduced firearm and total intimate partner homicide (Zeoli and Webster, 2010).

Most firearm-related deaths are suicides. Fifty percent of suicides are by firearm and 60 percent of firearm deaths are suicides (Law Center to Prevent Gun Violence, 2013). Research demonstrates that the proportion of suicide by firearm is greater in areas with higher household gun ownership (NRC, 2005). Further, two studies found "a small but significant fraction of gun suicides are committed within days to weeks after the purchase of a handgun, and both [studies] also indicate that gun purchasers have an elevated risk of suicide for many years after the purchase of the gun" (NRC, 2005, p. 181).

Social, Physical, and Virtual Environmental Interventions

Community Programs and Targeted Policing

Strengthened community policing and place-based interventions in certain "hotspots" have shown effective and compelling results in several places: Indianapolis, Kansas City, Missouri, and Pittsburgh are notable examples (NRC, 2005). Despite being well designed, however, evaluations of these interventions could not link all the changes to the programs. In addition, these interventions were limited, making long-term results difficult to predict.

Operation Cure Violence (previously referred to as CeaseFire) is a multicity, community-based violence prevention program that reaches out to gangs and other high-risk groups and individuals to interrupt disputes and violence (NIJ, 2008). Although not specific to firearm violence, Cure Violence has had some success in reducing overall violence in Chicago. In six of seven sites evaluated, attempted and actual shootings declined from 24 to 17 percent (Skogan et al., 2008). A meta-analysis by Arizona State University and the University of Cincinnati found that law enforcement efforts, such as place-based policing and probation with frequent contact with police, had more impact than prosecutorial policies, including stiff sentences (Makarios and Pratt, 2012).

In Boston, a problem-oriented "Gun Project" targeting serious youth offenders was implemented under the Cure Violence model. There was a significant decrease in homicides among youth, but the difficulty of controlling for all environmental factors that may have affected crime rates prevented a firm conclusion about exactly what contribution the interventions made (Fox and Zawitz, 2007). Effective place- and problem-oriented policing is aimed at all violence, not just firearm-related violence.

Regulations that limit the hours for on-premise alcohol sales in pubs, bars, and nightclubs have been associated with reduced violence. A quasi-experimental design based on data from Norwegian cities where the closing hours for on-premise alcohol sales were reduced demonstrated an impact on violence. For each additional hour of alcohol sales availability, violence increased by 16 percent (Rossow and Norstrom, 2012). Assault by firearm was 9.34 times more likely among heavy drinkers near off-premise alcohol points of sale than among nondrinkers in areas of low off-premise alcohol availability (Branas et al., 2009).

To date, there is little information about the potential role of mobile phone interventions or other electronic interventions in preventing firearm violence, although the combined use of mobile technology, including SMS (short message service) and GPS (global positioning system) has highlighted, in real time, the locations of violence against women in Cairo and Delhi (HarassMap, 2013).

Public Education and Warnings

Firearm safety education is intended to address the risk of unintentional injury and is particularly important when guns are kept in the home. Although firearm injury prevention education programs are widespread in public schools, they are inadequately studied and the few evaluations that have been conducted provide little evidence of effectiveness. It has been suggested that school-based prevention programs could actually glamorize guns among youth; however, information on childhood gun safety provided to parents by physicians may be effective (Dowd and Sege, 2012).

Regarding interventions for public mass shootings, there is no conclusive information about which policies and enforcement and prevention strategies might be effective. There have been analyses of these shootings (Bjelopera et al., 2013), but little has been done to compare them with those that were successfully averted. Although communities, schools, and campuses have developed myriad safety plans, there is very little information available about their effectiveness.

Community-based programs and targeted policing interventions in general have been found to be effective in reducing violence in some settings. Results of research on the effectiveness of prosecutorial interventions such as enhanced sentencing are weak. Controlling access to guns through background checks or restrictions on particular types of firearms remains controversial and requires additional research. Concerns about privacy regarding gun ownership, as well as individuals' mental health records, encumber data collection and research on firearm violence. The best way to protect children from unintentional firearm-related injuries remains elusive, but technology interventions appear to offer significant opportunities (see the section "Impact of Gun Safety Technology"). One study found a decrease in gun violence rates in Philadelphia by "greening" vacant lots, a community blight reduction strategy that may have enhanced informal policing by residents and reduced opportunities for the storage or disposal of illegal firearms (Branas et al., 2011).

Research Questions

There is limited research on the effectiveness of interventions and strategies to prevent firearm violence, and where there has been research, stakeholders often disagree about its implications. Two of the most challenging and important issues are the inadequacy of or lack of access to data (Weiner et al., 2007) and the use of study designs that have limited ability to establish causality. Data used in research on firearm violence are largely taken from datasets developed for other purposes. Methodological challenges include privacy and confidentiality concerns, noncomparability of datasets, definitional differences, and unreliability in self-reporting. The following four research topics were identified as priority areas:

Evaluate Interventions Aimed at Reducing Illegal Access and Possession of Firearms

Illegal access to and use of firearms is an important factor in our nation's risk from firearm violence. Fundamental questions about the effectiveness of interventions—both social and legal—remain unanswered.

Almost all guns used in criminal acts enter circulation via an initial legal transaction. Background checks at the point of sale may be effective at preventing illegal access to firearms, but these checks are not required for all gun sales or transfers. This, plus the fact that guns are frequently transported across state lines, despite provisions in the 1968 Gun Control Act,[33] may limit the effectiveness of the current system. The result of these inefficiencies is that illegal firearms are readily available to those with criminal intent. In 1998, 1,020 of 83,272 federally licensed retailers (1.2 percent) accounted for 57.4 percent of all guns traced by the ATF (Wintemute et al., 2005). Gun sales are also relatively concentrated; approximately 15 percent of retailers request 80 percent of background checks on gun buyers conducted by the National Instant Criminal Background Check System (NICS) (Wintemute et al., 2005). However, this information requires further study because Wintemute and colleagues (2005) also found that the share of crime gun traces attributed to these few dealers only slightly exceeded their share of handgun sales, which are almost equally concentrated among a few dealers.

Improve understanding of whether interventions intended to diminish the illegal carrying of firearms reduce firearm violence.

Examples of research questions that could be examined:

- What is the degree to which background checks at the point of sale are effective in deterring acquisition of firearms by those who are legally disqualified from owning one?
- What is the public health impact of removing firearms from persons who develop a disqualifying characteristic, for example, mental illness with potential for violence?
- Do programs that focus on changing norms in a community decrease illegal gun carrying?

Improve understanding of whether reducing criminal access to legally purchased guns reduces firearm violence.

Examples of topics that could be examined:

---

[33]Public Law 90-618, 82 Stat. 1213 (October 22, 1968).

- Are there methods to enhance the reporting of stolen guns in order to reduce illegal access?
- To what degree would mandatory reporting of transfer of private ownership of guns be effective in reducing illegal access?
- To what extent do focused interventions (e.g., "server training,"[34] straw-purchase[35] stings) targeted at high-risk retailers found to be disproportionately associated with gun crimes reduce illegal access?
- How do firearms move from federal firearms-licensed dealers to high-risk/criminal possessors? How can we develop detailed analyses of this illegal area of firearm distribution?

Evaluate Programs to Reduce Injuries by Legally Possessed Firearms

In 2010, there were approximately 19,000 suicides by firearm in the United States,[36] and 606 people were killed by a firearm unintentionally.[37] Thousands more were injured and survived with various degrees of disability. Stratifying risk among people with access to guns and reducing that risk may confer a public health benefit. The interaction of alcohol and gun use has been a subject of attention. There is an inconsistent patchwork of state laws to ameliorate the risk of firearm use by those that abuse alcohol. There is a lack of data on the basis for these laws or on their effectiveness

Risk stratification with respect to mental illness status and the use of firearms is imprecise and not well understood. Although the risk associated with certain specific psychiatric diagnoses is better understood than it has been in the past, conditions that foster a propensity toward violence

---

[34]Server training is an intervention used to provide staff of establishments that serve alcohol the knowledge and skills to ensure that they serve alcohol in a responsible manner and that they meet their legal responsibilities. Similar interventions may be used in firearm retail establishments.

[35]A "straw purchase" occurs when the buyer of a firearm would not pass required background checks or does not want his or her name associated with the purchase of the firearm and therefore uses someone else to make the actual purchase.

[36]NCIPC. 2013. *WISQARS injury mortality reports: 2010, United States, suicide firearm deaths and rates per 100,000—all races, both sexes, all ages* (accessed April 30, 2013).

[37]NCIPC. 2013. *WISQARS injury mortality reports: 2010, United States, unintentional firearm deaths and rates per 100,000—all races, both sexes, all ages* (accessed April 30, 2013).

and risk taking are not well defined and may not be noticed by authorities in a way that would trigger a prohibition of sale of a firearm.

Improve understanding of the effectiveness of actions directed at preventing access to firearms by violence-prone individuals.

Examples of topics that could be examined:

- What would be the effects of altering environmental alcohol availability, such as reducing the number of off-premise alcohol outlets, on firearm violence?
- How effective are policies and enforcement of laws preventing gun sales to people with specific psychiatric diagnoses?
- To what extent does enforcement of laws requiring removal of firearms from the homes of people with a history of intimate partner violence reduce homicide and injury?

Reduce Harm to Children and Youth

The risk to young people from firearms falls into three categories: self-injury, including suicide; harm to others, including homicide; and unintentional injury. Although the CDC has devoted significant efforts toward violence reduction, the interaction of guns and violent behavior reduction has not been a focus.

Unintentional firearm injury to children deserves special attention due to the uniquely vulnerable nature of this population, although these incidents are relatively infrequent compared with other types of firearm violence and thus do not constitute a large burden of disease. Young children cannot decide for themselves whether to live in a home with a firearm or whether to store weapons and ammunition safely. Much like other injury countermeasures designed with the vulnerability of children in mind (e.g., rear cameras in vehicles to reduce backover injuries), which have been mandated by Congress irrespective of disease burden, attention should be given to performing research that will inform how to protect this population. Rigorous studies evaluating youth intervention programs is also required to assess the benefits and impact on a youth's interest and comfort in carrying a firearm (Farah et al., 1999; Jackman et al., 2001).

Determine the degree to which various childhood education or prevention programs reduce firearm violence in childhood and later in life.

Examples of topics that could be examined:

- Are school-, family-, and community-based risk-reduction and health-promotion programs effective in reducing firearm violence?
- Are gun safety programs effective in reducing unintentional injury to children from firearms?
- Are school personnel (e.g., nurses, resource officers, teachers) effective at detecting students at risk of causing firearm violence?

Make High-Risk Environments Less Conducive to Firearm Violence

Improvements to the environment in "hotspot" areas, including remediation of vacant lots and abandoned buildings, has shown some promise (Branas et al., 2011) in reducing neighborhood firearm violence, but the reasons are not known. Conversely, high-risk neighborhoods with ready access to alcohol for off-premises consumption may face increased risk of alcohol-related violence (Branas et al., 2009). Programs known as "community policing" have resulted in decreased violence beyond arrest and enforcement effects (NRC, 2005).

Do programs to alter physical environments in high-crime areas result in a decrease in firearm violence?

Examples of topics that could be examined:

- Is there a correlation between alcohol sales for off-premises consumption and firearm violence in high-risk neighborhoods? Do laws and enforcement regarding sales of alcohol affect gun violence?
- What are the effects on firearm violence of community engagement programs to improve the physical environment? Is there a reduction in firearm violence among youth living in neighborhoods where community policing is practiced?

- For community programs that are considered to have sufficient effectiveness in reducing gun violence, what are the factors that affect adoption, fidelity vs. adaptation, and sustainability or scale-up of programs so that they have a public health impact?

IMPACT OF GUN SAFETY TECHNOLOGY

One technique that could be used to reduce the number of firearm-related injuries and deaths—intentional or unintentional—is to make guns safer. From a public health perspective, this would involve learning how to interrupt the connection between the agent (the gun or gun user), the host (victim), and the high-risk environment (Runyan, 1998). This is consistent with public health strategies to reduce the burden of product-related injuries, such as safety designs in cars and medicine (Hemenway and Miller, 2013). Research from the injury prevention field indicates that changing products to make them safer is frequently more effective at reducing injury and death than trying to change personal behavior (Teret and Culross, 2002, p. 120). For example, product-safety solutions to reduce childhood poisoning from medicines, such as changes in packaging, have resulted in fewer childhood deaths from medicinal poisoning. Similarly, making guns a safer consumer product would include design or technology improvements that reduce firearm-related deaths and injury.

Gun Technology Safety Features

The purpose of gun safety technologies is to prevent unintentional "shootings, usually by very young children; the shooting of police officers by assailants using the officers' own weapons; [and] suicides, especially by teenagers" (NAE, 2003, p. 2). In addition, in some cases this prevention strategy offers the prospect of reducing firearm-related crime by rendering a gun unusable to an unauthorized person.

Safety features in guns are not new. For example, Smith and Wesson firearm manufacturers developed a grip safety for children in the 1880s (Teret et al., 1998). There are both active and passive technologies that may have an impact. Passive technologies—for example, technologies that recognize person-specific features such as voice, hand geometry, iris scans, and fingerprints—are those that confer a safety benefit without requiring any specific action by a user. Active technologies require a specific action by a user to enable the technology—for example, to activate a firearm a user has to produce an item that activates the firearm (e.g., tokens, magnetic stripe badges, or proximity cards). Recently, gun safety technologies have focused on solutions that involve advanced technologies, passive, and person-specific approaches, such as "smart guns." The term "smart gun" is used as an overarching concept to cover all weapons that have some level of user authorization. Types of user authorization include technologies that require

- a user to provide information through mechanisms such as combinations, personal identification numbers, and passwords;
- a user to produce an item that activates the firearm—e.g., tokens, magnetic stripe badges, or proximity cards; or
- an individual recognition—e.g., technologies that recognize person-specific features such as voice, hand geometry, iris scans, and fingerprints (Weiss, 1996).

A personalized smart gun is defined as one that is designed to be fired only by an authorized user, automatically recognizes the user, automatically reverts to a locked state without requiring any overt action (beyond grasping or releasing the weapon), and can be programmed or reprogrammed for different users (Weiss, 1996).

Overview of Past and Ongoing Research on Gun Safety Technology

In 1994 and 2001, two studies commissioned by the National Institute of Justice (NIJ)[38] identified 14 potential user-authorized technologies for further exploration. Of those, radio frequency identification (RFID) was determined to be the most viable (Weiss, 1996; Wirsbinski, 2001), but biometric approaches have continued to be explored (see Table 1).

Biometric recognition technology involves the automated verification "of a living person in real time based on a physical characteristic" (Jaiswal et al., 2011, p. 20). These systems rely on recognition of a unique physical characteristic of an individual, such as face, voice, fingerprint, hand geometry, iris, retina, or DNA. Common applications of

---

[38]Although the research in this area began in order to address a risk to law enforcement, in subsequent years the deaths of police officers by their own weapons have decreased, possibly due to improved training, body armor, and secure holsters (FBI, 2011d).

this technology include ATMs, immigration and border control, fraud protection, privacy of medical records, physical access control, time and attendance records, computer security, telecommunications, and criminal investigations (Jain et al., 2012). Five biometric technologies may be effective in firearms; of those, only two may be adaptable to handguns (NAE, 2005).

Challenges to Developing Gun Safety Technologies

There are approximately 1,000 patents on record for various designs to prevent access to a firearm by unauthorized users, but many are untested. The patents address a range of unauthorized user prevention devices and methods, such as electronically activated holsters, firearm holster locks with fingerprint identification, audio-controlled gun-locking mechanisms, biometrically activated locks and enablement systems, voice-activated weapon-lock apparatuses, RFID, and various other designs (see Table 1) (PatentStorm, LLC, 2013). Barriers to development of these and other user-authorized technologies include lack of funding and standards:

- **Funding for smart-gun research** largely has come from the federal government, although New Jersey committed some state funding to support the work of the New Jersey Institute of Technology. Together, the state and federal money totaled approximately $12 million from 1994 to 2005, with no follow-up funding planned at that time. Despite the need for greater research, development efforts will be delayed without ongoing federal support or direct investments by gun manufacturers (NAE, 2005).
- **Safety standards for firearms** are not regulated by the Consumer Product Safety Commission due to a prohibition enacted in 1976 (Teret et al., 1998). Standards and regulations for smart-gun technology are important and consistent with President Obama's plan to protect our children and communities by reducing firearm violence (White House, 2013a).

In addition to these barriers, the development and application of smart-gun technologies have been complicated by problems such as recognition failures due to dirt on fingertips or the use of gloves, voices or body heat altered by stress, sweat interrupting direct connection with a device, and limited battery life. More work is needed to integrate fully functional technological solutions to particular prevention challenges, improve reliability, and ensure that these technologies are designed to reduce or eliminate the disabling of safety features by unauthorized users.

There is also the challenge of consumer acceptance and adoption of these safety measures. Safety features such as seat belts are sometimes disabled by the consumer, despite widespread public awareness of the risks. Individuals may also "offset the safety gains ... by reducing precautions or taking greater risks" (IOM, 1999, p. 122). Further, due to the costs associated with performing research on new technologies and the implementation of new technologies in the manufacturing of firearms, there is the potential for higher incurred costs by the gun purchasers that may also impact consumer adoption (NAE, 2003). Table 1 includes a broad range of conceivable gun safety technologies, without regard to current technological feasibility, cost, or consumer acceptance.

TABLE 1 Gun Safety Technology: Examples

Safety Mechanisms	Mechanical Mechanisms	Safety levers on weapons, push-button safeties, magazine disconnects, and firing pin blocks (widely available).
	External locking devices	Prevents the firing of a weapon through an external mechanism that encloses part of or the entire firearm, such as trigger locks, gun lockboxes, locking holsters, and personalized retention holsters or gun lockboxes that use biometrics (fingerprints) to identify authorized users (widely available).
	Key or combination lock	A lockable gun has an integrated or internal mechanism that prevents the locked firearm from being discharged until the user is recognized. A lockable gun requires an overt action by the user to both lock and unlock the firearm (once unlocked, the firearm can be fired by anyone until it is relocked). The locking mechanism may be mechanical, electromechanical, or electronic, such as a key, combination, or access-code technology using a pin number to activate the handgun (widely available).

"Smart" Technologies	**Radio frequency identification (RFID)**	Integrated data read by radio waves (similar to merchandise control tags commonly used in stores). Data could be stored in a variety of ways, such as on a magnetic strip or memory chip. An example for use in gun technology is embedding a data chip in a watch or ring, with a reader embedded in the firearm. The firearm "recognizes" the user via the data chip, the safety disengages, and the gun can be fired. When originally examined by Colt, the iGun technology was designed for long guns; the project has largely been abandoned. Another version of this approach, called TriggerSmart, is under development by the Georgia Institute of Technology in Ireland. A design feature under development, known as "wide area control," would allow a receiving device embedded in the firearm to be enabled or disabled remotely when entering designated areas, which has possible military application.
	Magnetic encoding	Magnetically locks mechanisms of the gun and will unlock when in close proximity to the magnetic device, such as a magnetic ring. Existing technology is commercially available as retrofit installations under trade names such as Magloc and Magna Trigger.
	Biometric systems	Automated devices that measure unique physical characteristics to identify and authenticate the authorized user. A number of different systems have been examined, including grip-pattern verification, fingerprint identification, and voice recognition. One system developed by the New Jersey Institute of Technology uses a grip-verification approach called Dynamic Grip Recognition.

Location awareness	Although still a theory and not currently under development, with a tracking device embedded in the firearm, GPS (global positioning system) technology could allow guns to know their own location and the location of other guns within a certain range. This has the potential, for example, to reduce unintentional injuries for hunters or intentional injuries of police officers by armed assailants.
Target recognition	Still a theory and not currently under development, target-sensing technology could prevent a gun from being fired if a child is within the target field.

SOURCES: Chen and Recce, 2007; NAE, 2005; Newcombe, 2013; Valenta et al., 2013; Weiss, 1996.

Current and Ongoing Research

Like past technologies that reduce injury, the development of "smart" or user-authorized guns has progressed and likely will have an impact on firearm violence. The research to date illustrates three common conclusions:

1. It is unlikely that one technology will address all circumstances and requirements.
2. Connecting particular technologies with specific scenarios is critical.
3. Technologies will always vary in simplicity, cost, effectiveness, and reliability.

The current state of smart-gun technology appears to be reaching a level of maturity at which private-industry adoption is important and necessary to move the technology to broader use. For example, a smart gun developed in Germany has been approved for importation to the United States (Bulwa, 2013; Teret, 2013). The committee did not determine the exact status of smart-gun technology, but instead focused on the potential public health benefits of such technological developments. A determination of the state of the technology is part of President Obama's 2013 executive orders to reduce firearm violence; a directive under Action #2 directs the attorney general to "issue a report on the availability and most effective use of new gun safety technologies and challenge the private sector to develop innovative technologies" (White House, 2013a, p. 10).

In addition to user-authorization technologies, there are active measures (requiring an overt action by the consumer, such as gun locks, gun safeties, and trigger locks) that responsible gun owners can use to reduce unauthorized access to firearms and help reduce firearm-related deaths (Grossman et al., 2005). Other technologies, such as less-than-lethal weaponry, video surveillance, micro-stamping of ammunition, and gunshot recognition systems using acoustics triangulation, were not considered by this committee. However, technologies that can reduce firearm violence are critically important to complement behavioral and population-level interventions.

Research Questions

Outstanding research questions include an examination of the most effective application of gun safety technology, the potential for general acceptance and usage of the safety features, and different policy approaches to implementation. In order to address the gaps in knowledge related to public health, the committee has identified three priority areas for research:

1. the effect of specific gun safety technologies on firearm-related injuries and deaths;
2. past consumer adoption lessons to address the challenge of consumer acceptance of gun safety features; and
3. the experiences of various states and countries with gun safety technology to identify effective methods for introducing and disseminating gun safety technologies.

The Effect of Specific Technological Approaches to Reducing Firearm-Related Injuries and Deaths

Injury prevention science has compared the strengths and limitations of various active strategies to control injuries and has found that passive strategies have a greater effect than attempts to change individual behavior (Teret and Culross, 2002). Therefore, passive strategies, such as personalized guns, show promise in reducing firearm violence and may have benefits across multiple public health contexts. In addition, passive strategies may also reduce the incidence of stolen guns and the resulting crimes (NAE, 2003). More data are needed to examine the potential impact of personalized guns in several areas of public health interest.

Identify the effects of different technological approaches to reduce firearm-related injury and death.

Examples of topics that could be examined:

- What is the projected impact of passive technologies on reduction of firearm violence, and which of the technologies will have the greatest impact on one or more of the types of harm from firearm violence (i.e., homicide, suicide, unintentional injury)?
  - o Are there feasible mechanisms to child-proof, and what is the projected impact of these technologies?
- How would potential technologies impact professional sectors (e.g., police and private security) in performing their duties effectively?
- How compliant would firearm owners be with safety technologies, or would owners disable technologies to assure their ability to use the firearms in an emergency?

Past Consumer Acceptance Experiences to Inform the Development and Dissemination of Gun Safety Technology

Previous successful injury prevention strategies have been informed by examining consumer acceptance challenges (Braitman et al., 2010). The integration of passive safety systems in cars, such as airbags, required many years of technology development as well as many years of public discussions before airbags became fully integrated and accepted in the United States. Improved understanding of how product safety measures are accepted and used at the population level is critical to ultimately achieving a reduction of preventable deaths and injuries related to firearms through gun safety technologies.

Examine past consumer experiences with accepting safety technologies to inform the development and uptake of new gun safety technologies.

Examples of topics that could be examined:

- Are there lessons from the adoption of other public health interventions involving passive technology improvements that could facilitate the acceptance and dissemination of passive gun safety technologies? Would consumer engagement accelerate acceptance and dissemination of gun safety technologies?
- What were the key factors that led to eventual population-level acceptance of various public safety technologies? Were these factors different for passive versus active technology changes? Were these factors different when active and passive technologies were combined?
- In previous product safety efforts, how long did it take for the safety feature to become reliable and how did that time frame impact consumer acceptance? Would this experience of timing and acceptance impact projections of gun safety technology implementation?
- To what extent did additional costs associated with safety features influence consumer acceptance and adoption?

State and International Experiences with Gun Safety and Technology

Another challenge is the implementation of new technologies through various policy mechanisms. There is a range of approaches being adopted by U.S. states and other countries, from mandating that all firearms sold include passive safety features immediately upon availability to requiring that all transfers of firearms include provision of a locking mechanism. Dissemination and adoption levels across states and countries for active strategies, such as gun locks and safeties, as well as for passive strategies, such as personalized guns, are largely unknown. Comparative analyses of state and international policy approaches to implementing active and passive gun safety strategies will improve the understanding of the impact of these interventions and help determine the resulting effect on rates of firearm-related injuries and deaths.

Explore individual state and international policy approaches to gun safety technology for applicability to the United States as a whole.

Examples of topics that could be examined:

- What can be learned from various state or international policy approaches to implementing passive and active gun technology changes, and what has been the impact of these changes on firearm violence?
    - What can be learned about the effects of these changes on the types of firearm-related injuries and deaths?
    - What was the impact of these approaches on consumer adoption and acceptance?
- What have been the adoption rates and effectiveness of active protection technologies among law enforcement users?

However, cross-national comparisons, as suggested here, are susceptible to large ecological biases and unmeasured confounding biases, and therefore conclusions from these studies may not apply to individuals.

VIDEO GAMES AND OTHER MEDIA

Although research on the effects of media violence on real-life violence has been carried out for more than 50 years (Cook et al., 1983; Eron and Huesmann, 1980; Eron et al., 1972; Huesmann, 1986; Huesmann and Miller, 1994; Huesmann et al., 2003; McIntyre et al., 1972; Milavsky et al., 1982; Robinson and Bachman, 1972; Rubenstein, 1983; Surgeon General's Scientific Advisory Committee on Television and Social Behavior, 1972), little of this research has focused on real-life firearm violence in particular (Boxer et al., 2009; Huesmann et al., 2003; Ybarra et al., 2008). As a result, a direct relationship between media violence and real-life firearm violence has not been established. Although the bulk of past media violence research has focused on violence portrayed in television and film, more recent research has expanded to include music, video games, social media, and the Internet. Interest in media effects is fueled by the fact that youth spend an increasing amount of time engaging with media. The most recent estimates indicate that 8- to 18-year-olds in the United States spend an average of 7.5 hours per day using entertainment media, including television, movies, music, cell phones, video games, and the Internet (Kaiser Family Foundation, 2010). Media content is also a concern: more than 800 violent acts are shown on television each hour in the United States; about 15 percent of music videos portray interpersonal violence (Beresin, 2010); and two-thirds of the 97 percent of children who play video games play games that may include violence (Lenhart et al., 2008). However, data on the prevalence of firearm violence in the media are absent. The following section reviews potential associations of exposure to media violence and violent acts, but is not specific to firearm violence.

Overview of Past and Ongoing Research on Media Violence and Violent Acts

Short-Term Experimental Studies on Exposure to Media Violence

The vast majority of research on the effects of media violence is based on short-term laboratory or field experiments. These studies examine short-term effects of media exposure on physical and verbal aggressive behavior, thoughts, and emotions; hostility; fearful behaviors; physiological arousal (e.g., changes in heart rate); the tendency to mimic behavior; and changes in helpful behaviors, empathy, and pro-social behaviors in both males and females (Anderson, 2004; Anderson and Bushman, 2001; Anderson and Dill, 2000; Anderson et al., 2003, 2010; Bartholow et al., 2005; Browne and Hamilton-Giachritsis, 2005; Bushman and Huesmann, 2006; Fuld et al., 2009). Fewer studies examine the link between short-term exposure to media violence and violent behaviors such as arguing, fighting, aggravated or sexual assault, shooting, stabbing, and robbery (Gentile et al., 2004; Ybarra et al., 2008).

These short-term experimental studies consistently document significant effects of experimentally manipulated media exposure on a wide range of short-term outcomes. Results are broadly similar in studies of television and film violence (Bandura et al., 1963; Bushman and Huesmann, 2001; Huesmann et al., 2000; Paik and Comstock, 1994; Wood et al., 1991) and violent video games (Anderson, 2004; Anderson and Bushman, 2001; Anderson and Dill, 2000; Bartholow et al., 2005; Gentile et al., 2004). However, effects vary as a complex function of interactions among media content, viewer characteristics, and social contexts (Anderson et al., 2003) and are open to a number of interpretations other than those favored by the majority of researchers in the area, such as the suggestion that portrayals of competitiveness, rather than violence, account for these negative effects of media exposure (Adachi and Willoughby, 2011a,b; Przybylski et al., 2010).

Copycat Behaviors as a Result of Media Violence

Some research suggests that media violence may be imitated or copied in real life, especially in cases of suicide (which may or may not involve a gun) (Bollen and Phillips, 1982; Chen et al., 2012; Gould et al., 2003; Phillips, 1982; Pirkis et al., 2006; Stack, 2003, 2005; Tousignant et al., 2005). Research has shown an increase in suicide attempts after the publicized suicide of a political or entertainment celebrity (Chen et al., 2012; Stack, 2003, 2005; Tousignant et al., 2005), as well as publicity surrounding mass suicides or murder-suicides (Pirkis et al., 2006). A dose–response relationship has also been documented between the intensity of media exposure and the number of subsequent presumably copycat suicides (Etzersdorfer et al., 2001). Evidence has also been found for consistencies between the methods of suicide detailed in media stories and presumably imitative suicides that occur in the wake of media stories (Etzersdorfer et al., 2001; Tousignant et al., 2005), adding to the plausibility of the interpretation that these events are copied. Research has also shown that the strength of effects on presumably imitative suicides varies by type of media, with television publicity sometimes seeming to result in more suicide imitators (Pirkis et al., 2006) and sometimes fewer (Stack, 2003, 2005) than if the suicide was publicized in newspapers.

Although there is not much research in this area, the existing research on broad patterns of presumably copycat acts is sufficiently strong to suggest that it might be useful to carry out more in-depth studies, such as retrospective case-control psychological autopsy studies, in an effort to learn more about the characteristics of people who are susceptible to such media effects and determine if there are any modifiable risk factors that could provide insights on effective preventive interventions. Such in-depth studies might also produce insights that could advise media purveyors about changes in frequency or type of violent content to help reduce copycat effects or encourage help-seeking behaviors (Pirkis et al., 2006; Stack, 2003).

In addition to concerns about direct imitations of media violence, there are other possible adverse effects of media stories such as evening news reports about violent incidents in the community and ongoing sensationalized stories about high-profile murders and mass shootings (i.e., the "mean world syndrome" [Gerbner et al., 1980, 1986]). Some evidence exists that these types of news stories are associated with unrealistic perceptions of low community safety (Chiricos et al., 2000; Ditton et al., 2004; O'Keefe, 1984) as well as, in some cases, secondhand trauma-related fear, depression, feelings of vulnerability, and PTSD (Ahern et al., 2002; Bernstein et al., 2007; Comer et al., 2008; Fremont et al., 2005; Otto et al., 2007; Saylor et al., 2003). The extent to which high exposure to such stories leads to changes in proneness to violence for the exposed individuals, though, has not been the subject of systematic research.

Longer-Term Longitudinal Studies in Youth on Exposure to Media Violence

A number of longitudinal studies document long-term associations between violent media exposure in childhood and the later occurrence of real-life aggression or violence (Anderson et al., 2010; Boxer et al., 2009; Browne and Hamilton-Giachritsis, 2005; Eron and Huesmann, 1980; Eron et al., 1972; Huesmann, 1996; 2007; Huesmann and Taylor, 2006; Huesmann et al., 1984; Krahé and Möller, 2010; Savage, 2004; Savage and Yancey, 2008; Slater et al., 2003). Some studies have shown that children who favor violent television, movies, or video games or who are heavily exposed to these types of media have elevated rates of later aggression and violence, such as bullying, physical fights, spousal abuse, responding to insults with violence, committing and being convicted of crimes, violent delinquency, and committing moving traffic violations (Anderson et al., 2008; Hopf et al., 2008; Huesmann et al., 2003; Olson et al., 2009). However, the fact that these studies are nonexperimental introduces uncertainties in interpreting the associations they document because of the possibility that unmeasured common causes could account for the associations. Advocates of a causal interpretation of these associations have argued that a causal link is indirectly supported by evidence of dose–response relationships between the magnitude of exposure and subsequent violence (Anderson and Dill, 2000; Anderson et al., 2008; Huesmann et al., 2003) and by the fact that associations persist after introducing statistical controls for plausible confounders (Anderson et al., 2008, 2010; Huesmann et al., 2003; Olson et al., 2009). However, the adequacy of these controls has been disputed by critics (Ferguson, 2011; Ferguson et al., 2008, 2012; Savage, 2004).

Causal interpretations of long-term associations between habitual exposure to media violence and later real-life violence are based on the observational learning process (Carroll and Bandura, 1987) that media violence leads to children learning long-term "aggressive scripts, interpretational schemas, and aggression-supporting beliefs about social behavior" (Anderson et al., 2003, p. 8) that result in more aggressive personalities (Anderson and Bushman, 2001; Bushman and Huesmann, 2006). Children observe others behaving violently, encode scripts for behaving violently themselves, and encode beliefs that violence is normal, increasing the risk that they will act aggressively or violently. Some studies suggest that repeated exposure to media violence may result in desensitization or a decrease in negative emotional response to violence (Anderson et al., 2003, 2010; Bartholow et al., 2005, 2006; Carnagey and Anderson, 2004; Carnagey et al., 2007; Fuld et al., 2009; Funk et al., 2004; Krahé et al., 2011), thereby reducing psychological barriers to committing violent acts. These theories are in line with some naturalistic specifications of the long-term associations documented in studies, such as the finding that associations are stronger for children than for adults (Bushman and Huesmann, 2006). As previously discussed, some mass murders may in fact be suicides preceded by mass murders. It is not, however, understood if media reporting events such as the ones that occurred in Columbine High School; Platte Canyon High School; an Amish school in Nickel Mines, Pennsylvania; Virginia Tech; and Northern Illinois may inadvertently promote these behaviors (IOM, 2013). Further, no experimental or quasi-experimental research (only research based on observational longitudinal and survey studies) has been carried out to provide definitive evidence that the long-term associations are causal rather than due to unmeasured common causes that select violence-prone youth into high levels of exposure to media violence. However, data from existing studies have shown that long-term associations cannot be solely explained by these unmeasured common causes.

Research Question

The limited evidence reviewed above is quite clear in arguing that significant relationships exist between violent media exposure and some measures of aggression and violent behavior. For example, it seems clear that there is a relationship between news stories of suicide and imitative suicides. The experimental literature is also very convincing in documenting effects of short episodes of violent media exposure on short-term outcomes, although, as noted above, some question the assumption that it is the violence of the media content that is the active component in these effects (Adachi and Willoughby, 2011a,b; Przybylski et al., 2010). There is also controversy about the extent to which evidence of such short-term effects is relevant to the long-term associations found between persistent violent media exposure in youth and subsequent real-life violence (Browne and Hamilton-Giachritsis, 2005; Ferguson, 2011; Ferguson et al., 2013; Savage, 2004); the absence of experimental data renders it impossible to make unequivocal interpretations of these long-term associations (Ferguson, 2009; Grimes et al., 2008; Gunter and Daly, 2012). Critics note additional limitations of studies documenting long-term associations between violent media exposure and real-life violence, including poorly validated outcome measures and inconsistent measures across studies of aggression, childhood media exposure, and later violence (Ferguson, 2011; Ferguson and Kilburn, 2009; Kutner and Olson, 2008; Savage, 2004).

The number and variety of long-term prospective studies are sufficient to warrant systematic parallel secondary analyses to address criticisms regarding appropriateness of measures and adequacy of controls. Appropriateness of measures could be addressed by sensitivity analyses to examine variation in results, based on recoding the baseline measures of media exposure and refining outcomes to focus on the subset of violent behaviors with more public health significance. Concerns about adequacy of controls in original analyses could be addressed by applying consistent methods of control analysis using modern statistical methods for supporting causal inferences based on non-experimental data.

Examine the relationship between exposure to media violence and real-life violence.

Examples of topics that could be examined:

- Synthesize evidence from existing studies and relevant databases that would reveal long-term associations between violent media exposure in childhood and subsequent adolescent or adult firearm-related violence. Studies should focus on evidence regarding the consistency and strength of these associations and the sensitivity of effect-size estimates.

- o Is there a relationship between long-term exposure to media violence and subsequent firearm-related violence? To what degree do violence-prone individuals disproportionately expose themselves to media violence?
- o If such a relationship exists, is it causal and who is most susceptible?
- o If a plausible case can be made that the relationship is causal, what kinds of people are most susceptible to the effects of media violence?
- o If the relationship is causal, which dimensions of media exposure are driving the relationship (e.g., competitiveness, violence, particular violence subtypes or contexts)?
- o Are the magnitude and consistency of the plausibly causal relationship sufficient to suggest a public health research agenda on interventions related to media violence?

A

References

Abrams, D. 2012. Estimating the deterrent effect of incarceration using sentencing enhancements. *American Economic Journal: Applied Economics* 4(4):32-56.

Adachi, P. J. C., and T. Willoughby. 2011a. The effect of video game competition and violence on aggressive behavior: Which characteristic has the greatest influence? *Psychology of Violence* 1(4):259-274.

Adachi, P. J. C., and T. Willoughby. 2011b. The effect of violent video games on aggression: Is it more than just the violence? *Aggression and Violent Behavior* 16(1):55-62.

Ahern, J., S. Galea, H. Resnick, D. Kilpatrick, M. Bucuvalas, J. Gold, and D. Vlahov. 2002. Television images and psychological symptoms after the September 11 terrorist attacks. *Psychiatry* 65(4):289-300.

Akers, T. A., and M. M. Lanier. 2009. Epidemiological criminology: Coming full circle. *American Journal of Public Health* 99(3):397-402.

Akers, T. A., R. H. Potter, and C. V. Hill. 2013. *Epidemiological Criminology: A Public Health Approach to Crime and Violence.* San Francisco, CA: Jossey-Bass.

Anderson, C. A. 2004. An update on the effects of playing violent video games. *Journal of Adolescence* 27(1):113-122.

Anderson, C. A., and B. J. Bushman. 2001. Effects of violent video games on aggressive behavior, aggressive cognition, aggressive affect, physiological arousal, and prosocial behavior: A meta-analytic review of the scientific literature. *Psychological Science* 12(5):353-359.

Anderson, C. A., and K. E. Dill. 2000. Video games and aggressive thoughts, feelings, and behavior in the laboratory and in life. *Journal of Personality and Social Psychology* 78(4):772-790.

Anderson, C. A., W. E. Deuser, and K. M. DeNeve. 1995. Hot temperatures, hostile affect, hostile cognition, and arousal: Tests of a general model of affective aggression. *Personality and Social Psychology Bulletin* 21(5):434-448.

Anderson, C. A., A. J. Benjamin, Jr., and B. D. Bartholow. 1998. Does the gun pull the trigger? Automatic priming effects of weapon pictures and weapon names. *Psychological Science* 9(4):308-314.

Anderson, C. A., L. Berkowitz, E. Donnerstein, L. R. Huesmann, J. D. Johnson, D. Linz, N. M. Malamuth, and E. Wartella. 2003. The influence of media violence on youth. *Psychological Science in the Public Interest, Supplement* 4(3):1-30.

Anderson, C. A., A. Sakamoto, D. A. Gentile, N. Ihori, A. Shibuya, S. Yukawa, M. Naito, and K. Kobayashi. 2008. Longitudinal effects of violent video games on aggression in Japan and the United States. *Pediatrics* 122(5): e1067-e1072.

Anderson, C. A., A. Shibuya, N. Ihori, E. L. Swing, B. J. Bushman, A. Sakamoto, H. R. Rothstein, and M. Saleem. 2010. Violent video game effects on aggression, empathy, and prosocial behavior in Eastern and Western countries: A meta-analytic review. *Psychological Bulletin* 136(2):151-173.

ATF (Bureau of Alcohol, Tobacco, Firearms and Explosives). 2011. *Firearms tracing guide: Tracing firearms to reduce violent crime.* Washington, DC: Bureau of Alcohol, Tobacco, Firearms and Explosives. http://www. atf.gov/files/publications/download/p/atf-p-3312-13.pdf (accessed April 17, 2013).

ATF. 2012. *Firearms commerce in the United States: Annual statistical update, 2012.* Washington, DC: Bureau of Alcohol, Tobacco, Firearms and Explosives. http://www.atf.gov/files/publications/firearms/050412-firearms-commerce-in-the-us-annual-statistical-update-2012.pdf (accessed April 8, 2013).

Bandura, A., D. Ross, and S. A. Ross. 1963. Imitation of film-mediated aggressive models. *Journal of Abnormal and Social Psychology* 66(1):3-11.

Bartholow, B. D., M. A. Sestir, and E. B. Davis. 2005. Correlates and consequences of exposure to video game violence: Hostile personality, empathy, and aggressive behavior. *Personality and Social Psychology Bulletin* 31(11):1573-1586.

Bartholow, B. D., B. J. Bushman, and M. A. Sestir. 2006. Chronic violent video game exposure and desensitization to violence: Behavioral and event-related brain potential data. *Journal of Experimental Social Psychology* 42(4):532-539.

Beaman, V., J. L. Annest, J. A. Mercy, M. J. Kresnow, and D. A. Pollock. 2000. Lethality of firearm-related injuries in the United States population. *Annals of Emergency Medicine* 35(3):258-266.

Bell, C. C., and D. F. McBride. 2010. Commentary: Homicide-suicide in older adults—cultural and contextual perspectives. *Journal of the American Academy of Psychiatry and the Law* 38(3):312-317.

Beresin, E. V. 2010. *The impact of media violence on children and adolescents: Opportunities for clinical interventions.* http://www.aacap.org/cs/root/developmentor/the_impact_of_media_violence_on_children_and_adol-escents_opportunities_for_clinical_interventions (accessed March 22, 2013).

Berkowitz, L., and A. LePage. 1967. Weapons as aggressive-eliciting stimuli. *Journal of Personality and Social Psychology* 7(2, Pt 1):202-207.

Bernstein, K. T., J. Ahern, M. Tracy, J. A. Boscarino, D. Vlahov, and S. Galea. 2007. Television watching and the risk of incident probable posttraumatic stress disorder: A prospective evaluation. *Journal of Nervous and Mental Disease* 195(1):41-47.

Bingenheimer, J. B., R. T. Brennan, and F. J. Earls. 2005. Firearm violence exposure and serious violent behavior. *Science* 308(5726):1323-1326.

Bjelopera, J. P., E. Bagalman, S. W. Caldwell, K. M. Finklear, and G. McCallion. 2013. *Public mass shootings in the United States: Selected implications for federal public health and safety policy.* Washington, DC: Congressional Research Service. http://www.fas.org/sgp/crs/misc/R43 004.pdf (accessed April 8, 2013).

BJS (Bureau of Justice Statistics). 2010. *Criminal victimization in the United States, 2008: Statistical tables, NCJ 231173.* Washington, DC: BJS. http://bjs.gov/content/pub/pdf/cvus08.pdf (accessed April 29, 2013).

Blumstein, A. 1995. Youth violence, guns, and the illicit-drug industry. *Journal of Criminal Law & Criminology* 86(1):10-36.

Blumstein, A., and D. Cork. 1996. Linking gun availability to youth gun violence. *Law and Contemporary Problems* 59(1):5-24.

Bollen, K. A., and D. P. Phillips. 1982. Imitative suicides: A national study of the effects of television news stories. *American Sociological Review* 47(6):802-809.

Boxer, P., L. Rowell Huesmann, B. J. Bushman, M. O'Brien, and D. Moceri. 2009. The role of violent media preference in cumulative developmental risk for violence and general aggression. *Journal of Youth and Adolescence* 38(3):417-428.

Braitman, K. A., A. T. McCartt, D. S. Zuby, and J. Singer. 2010. Volvo and Infiniti drivers' experiences with select crash avoidance technologies. *Traffic Injury Prevention* 11(3):270-278.

Branas, C. C., M. L. Nance, M. R. Elliott, T. S. Richmond, and C. W. Schwab. 2004. Urban-rural shifts in intentional firearm death: Different causes, same results. *American Journal of Public Health* 94(10):1750-1755.

Branas, C. C., M. R. Elliott, T. S. Richmond, D. P. Culhane, and D. J. Wiebe. 2009. Alcohol consumption, alcohol outlets, and the risk of being assaulted with a gun. *Alcoholism, Clinical and Experimental Research* 33(5):906-915.

Branas, C. C., R. A. Cheney, J. M. MacDonald, V. W. Tam, T. D. Jackson, and T. R. Ten Have. 2011. A difference-in-differences analysis of health, safety, and greening vacant urban space. *American Journal of Epidemiology* 174(11):1296-1306.

Browne, K. D., and C. Hamilton-Giachritsis. 2005. The influence of violent media on children and adolescents: A public-health approach. *Lancet* 365(9460):702-710.

Buka, S. L., T. L. Stichick, I. Birdthistle, and F. J. Earls. 2001. Youth exposure to violence: Prevalence, risks, and consequences. *American Journal of Orthopsychiatry* 71(3):298-310.

Bulwa, D. 2013. *Personalized guns touted as safety check.* http://www.sfgate.com/nation/article/Personalized-guns-touted-as-safety-check-4323902.php (accessed April 30, 2013).

Bushman, B. J., and L. R. Huesmann. 2001. Effects of televised violence on aggression. In *Handbook of Children and the Media*, edited by D. G. Singer and J. L. Singer. Thousand Oaks, CA: Sage. Pp. 223-254.

Bushman, B. J., and L. R. Huesmann. 2006. Short-term and long-term effects of violent media on aggression in children and adults. *Archives of Pediatrics and Adolescent Medicine* 160(4):348-352.

Butke, P., and S. C. Sheridan. 2010. An analysis of the relationship between weather and aggressive crime in Cleveland, Ohio. *Weather, Climate, and Society* 2:127-139.

Carnagey, N. L., and C. A. Anderson. 2004. Violent video game exposure and aggression: A literature review. *Minerva Psichiatrica* 45(1):1-18.

Carnagey, N. L., C. A. Anderson, and B. J. Bushman. 2007. The effect of video game violence on physiological desensitization to real-life violence. *Journal of Experimental Social Psychology* 43(3):489-496.

Carr, B. G., M. L. Nance, C. C. Branas, C. S. Wolff, M. J. Kallan, S. R. Myers, and D. J. Wiebe. 2012. Unintentional firearm death across the urban-rural landscape in the United States. *Journal of Trauma and Acute Care Surgery* 73(4):1006-1010.

Carroll, W. R., and A. Bandura. 1987. Translating cognition into action: The role of visual guidance in observational learning. *Journal of Motor Behavior* 19(3):385-398.

CDC (Centers for Disease Control and Prevention). 2011a. *Injury prevention & control data: Data & statistics (WISQARS^{TM}): Fatal injury data.* http://www.cdc.gov/injury/wisqars/fatal.html (accessed April 29, 2013).

CDC. 2011b. *Youth violence: Risk and protective factors.* http://www.cdc.gov/violenceprevention/youthviolence/riskprotectivefactors.html (accessed April April 29, 2013).

CDC. 2012a. *Suicide: Facts at a glance.* http://www.cdc.gov/violenceprevention/pdf/Suicide_DataSheet-a.pdf (accessed April 29, 2013).

CDC. 2012b. Youth risk behavior surveillance—United States, 2011. *Morbidity and Mortality Weekly Report* (4). http://www.cdc.gov/mmwr/pdf/ss/ss6104.pdf (accessed April 30, 2013).

CDC. 2013a. *National Violent Death Reporting System.* http://www.cdc.gov/violenceprevention/nvdrs (accessed April 29, 2013).

CDC. 2013b. *National suicide statistics at a glance: Case fatality rate among persons ages 10 years and older for males and females separately, and by selected mechanism for both sexes combined, United States, 2005-2009.* http://www.cdc.gov/violenceprevention/suicide/statistics/case_fatality.html (accessed April 29, 2013).

Champion, H. L. O., and R. H. DuRant. 2001. Exposure to violence and victimization and the use of violence by adolescents in the United States. *Minerra Pediatrica* 53(3):189-197.

Chen, Y. Y., S. F. Liao, P. R. Teng, C. W. Tsai, H. F. Fan, W. C. Lee, and A. T. Cheng. 2012. The impact of media reporting of the suicide of a singer on suicide rates in Taiwan. *Social Psychiatry and Psychiatric Epidemiology* 47(2):215-221.

Chen, Z., and M. Recce. 2007. Handgrip recognition. *Journal of Engineering, Computing and Architecture* (2). http://www.scientificjournals.org/journals2007/articles/1226.pdf (accessed April 10, 2013).

Chiricos, T., K. Padgett, and M. Gertz. 2000. Fear, TV news, and the reality of crime. *Criminology* 38(3):755-785.

Comer, J. S., J. M. Furr, R. S. Beidas, H. M. Babyar, and P. C. Kendall. 2008. Media use and children's perceptions of societal threat and personal vulnerability. *Journal of Clinical Child and Adolescent Psychology* 37(3):622-630.

Conner, K. R., P. R. Duberstein, Y. Conwell, and E. D. Caine. 2003. Reactive aggression and suicide—theory and evidence. *Aggression and Violent Behavior* 8(4):413-432.

Cook, P. J., and J. Ludwig. 1996. *Guns in America: Results of a comprehensive survey on private firearms ownership and use.* Washington, DC: Police Foundation. http://www.policefoundation.org/sites/pftest1.drupalgardens.com/files/ Cook%20et%20al.%20%281996%29%20-%20Guns%20in%20America.pdf (accessed April 17, 2013).

Cook, P. J., J. Ludwig, and D. Hemenway. 1997. The gun debate's new mythical number: How many defensive uses per year? *Journal of Policy Analysis and Management* 16(3):463-469.

Cook, T. D., D. A. Kendzierski, and S. V. Thomas. 1983. The implicit assumptions of television research: An analysis of the 1982 NIMH report on television and behavior. *Public Opinion Quarterly* 47(2):161-201.

Cooper, A., and E. L. Smith. 2011. *Homicide trends in the United States, 1980-2008, NCJ 236018.* Washington, DC: Bureau of Justice Statistics. http://bjs.gov/content/pub/pdf/htus8008.pdf (accessed April 8, 2013).

Cunningham, P. B., S. W. Henggeler, S. P. Limber, G. B. Melton, and M. A. Nation. 2000. Patterns and correlates of gun ownership among nonmetropolitan and rural middle school students. *Journal of Clinical Child Psychology* 29(3):432-442.

Cusimano, M., S. Marshall, C. Rinner, D. Jiang, and M. Chipman. 2010. Patterns of urban violent injury: A spatio-temporal analysis. *PLoS ONE* 5(1):e8669.

Ditton, J., D. Chadee, S. Farrall, E. Gilchrist, and J. Bannister. 2004. From imitation to intimidation: A note on the curious and changing relationship between the media, crime and fear of crime. *British Journal of Criminology* 44(4):595-610.

Dowd, M. D., and R. D. Sege. 2012. Firearm-related injuries affecting the pediatric population. *Pediatrics* 130(5):e1416-e1423.

Ehrensaft, M. K., P. Cohen, J. Brown, E. Smailes, H. Chen, and J. G. Johnson. 2003. Intergenerational transmission of partner violence: A 20-year prospective study. *Journal of Consulting and Clinical Psychology* 71(4):741-753.

Elgar, F. J., and N. Aitken. 2011. Income inequality, trust and homicide in 33 countries. *European Journal of Public Health* 21(2):241-246.

Eron, L. D., and L. R. Huesmann. 1980. Adolescent aggression and television. *Annals of the New York Academy of Sciences* 347:319-331.

Eron, L. D., L. R. Huesmann, M. M. Lefkowitz, and L. O. Walder. 1972. Does television violence cause aggression? *American Psychologist* 27(4):253-263.

Etzersdorfer, E., M. Voracek, and G. Sonneck. 2001. A dose-response relationship of imitational suicides with newspaper distribution. *Australian and New Zealand Journal of Psychiatry* 35(2):251.

Farah, M. M., H. K. Simon, and A. L. Kellermann. 1999. Firearms in the home: Parental perceptions. *Pediatrics* 104(5 Pt 1):1059-1063.

FBI (Federal Bureau of Investigation). 2011a. *Crime in the United States, 2010: Table 1*. http://www.fbi.gov/about-us/cjis/ucr/crime-in-the-u.s/2010/crime-in-the-u.s.-2010/tables/10tbl01.xls (accessed May 8, 2013).

FBI. 2011b. *Crime in the United States, 2011: Expanded homicide data table 8*. http://www.fbi.gov/about-us/cjis/ucr/crime-in-the-u.s/2011/crime-in-the-u.s.-2011/tables/expanded-homicide-data-table-8 (accessed April 8, 2013).

FBI. 2011c. *Crime in the United States, 2010: Expanded offense data*. http://www.fbi.gov/about-us/cjis/ucr/crime-in-the-u.s/2010/crime-in-the-u.s.-2010/offenses-known-to-law-enforcement/expanded (accessed May 1, 2013).

FBI. 2011d. *Law enforcement officers killed and assaulted 2011: Table 14, Law enforcement officers feloniously killed with their own weapons—victim officer's type of weapon, 2002-2011*. http://www.fbi.gov/about-us/cjis/ucr/leoka/2011/tables/table-14 (accessed April 10, 2013).

Ferguson, C. J. 2009. Media violence effects: Confirmed truth or just another X-file? *Journal of Forensic Psychology Practice* 9(2):103-126.

Ferguson, C. J. 2011. Video games and youth violence: A prospective analysis in adolescents. *Journal of Youth and Adolescence* 40(4):377-391.

Ferguson, C. J., and J. Kilburn. 2009. The public health risks of media violence: A meta-analytic review. *Journal of Pediatrics* 154(5):759-763.

Ferguson, C. J., S. M. Rueda, A. M. Cruz, D. E. Ferguson, S. Fritz, and S. M. Smith. 2008. Violent video games and aggression: Causal relationship or byproduct of family violence and intrinsic violence motivation? *Criminal Justice and Behavior* 35(3):311-332.

Ferguson, C. J., C. San Miguel, A. Garza, and J. M. Jerabeck. 2012. A longitudinal test of video game violence influences on dating and aggression: A 3-year longitudinal study of adolescents. *Journal of Psychiatric Research* 46(2):141-146.

Ferguson, C. J., A. Garza, J. Jerabeck, R. Ramos, and M. Galindo. 2013. Not worth the fuss after all? Cross-sectional and prospective data on violent video game influences on aggression, visuospatial cognition and mathematics ability in a sample of youth. *Journal of Youth and Adolescence* 42(1):109-122.

Finkelhor, D., H. Turner, R. Ormrod, S. Hamby, and K. Kracke. 2009. *Children's exposure to violence: A comprehensive national survey*. Washington, DC: Office of Juvenile Delinquency Prevention. https://www.ncjrs.gov/pdffiles1/ojjdp/227744.pdf (accessed May 8, 2013).

Fitzpatrick, K. M. 1997. Aggression and environmental risk among low-income African-American youth. *Journal of Adolescent Health* 21(3):172-178.

Fleegler, E. W., L. K. Lee, M. C. Monuteaux, D. Hemenway, and R. Mannix. 2013. Firearm legislation and firearm-related fatalities in the United States. *JAMA Internal Medicine*. [Epub ahead of print]. http://archinte.jamanetwork.com/article.aspx?articleid=1661390 (accessed May 8, 2013).

Fowler, P. J., C. J. Tompsett, J. M. Braciszewski, A. J. Jacques-Tiura, and B. B. Baltes. 2009. Community violence: A meta-analysis on the effect of exposure and mental health outcomes of children and adolescents. *Development and Psychopathology* 21(1):227-259.

Fox, J. A., and M. W. Zawitz. 2007. *Homicide trends in the United States*. Washington, DC: Bureau of Justice Statistics. http://bjs.gov/content/pub/pdf/htius.pdf (accessed April 8, 2013).

Fremont, W. P., C. Pataki, and E. V. Beresin. 2005. The impact of terrorism on children and adolescents: Terror in the skies, terror on television. *Child and Adolescent Psychiatric Clinics of North America* 14(3):429-451.

Fuld, G. L., D. A. Mulligan, T. R. Altmann, A. Brown, D. A. Christakis, K. Clarke-Pearson, B. P. Dreyer, H. L. Falik, K. G. Nelson, G. S. O'Keeffe, V. C. Strasburger, R. M. Milteer, D. L. Shifrin, M. Brody, B. Wilcox, C. A. Anderson, D. A. Gentile, G. L. Steiner, and V. L. Noland. 2009. Policy statement—media violence. *Pediatrics* 124(5):1495-1503.

Funk, J. B., H. B. Baldacci, T. Pasold, and J. Baumgardner. 2004. Violence exposure in real-life, video games, television, movies, and the Internet: Is there desensitization? *Journal of Adolescence* 27(1):23-39.

Gallup. 2013. *Guns*. http://www.gallup.com/poll/1645/Guns.aspx (accessed April 8, 2013).

Garbarino, J., C. P. Bradshaw, and J. A. Vorrasi. 2002. Mitigating the effects of gun violence on children and youth. *Future Child* 12(2):72-85.

Gentile, D. A., P. J. Lynch, J. R. Linder, and D. A. Walsh. 2004. The effects of violent video game habits on adolescent hostility, aggressive behaviors, and school performance. *Journal of Adolescence* 27(1):5-22.

Gerbner, G., L. Gross, M. Morgan, and N. Signorielli. 1980. The "mainstreaming" of America: Violence profile no. 11. *Journal of Communication* 30(3):10-29.

Gerbner, G., L. Gross, M. Morgan, and N. Signorielli. 1986. Living with television: The dynamics of the cultivation process. In *Perspectives on Media Effects*, edited by J. Bryant and D. Zillmann. Hillsdale, NJ: Lawrence Erlbaum Associates. Pp. 17-40.

Gibbons, R. D., C. H. Brown, and K. Hur. 2012. Is the rate of suicide among veterans elevated? *American Journal of Public Health* 102(Suppl 1):S17-S19.

Goldstein, P. J. 1985. The drugs/violence nexus: A tripartite conceptual framework. *Journal of Drug Issues* 15(4):493-506.

Gould, M., P. Jamieson, and D. Romer. 2003. Media contagion and suicide among the youth. *American Behavioral Scientist* 46(9):1269-1284.

Greenberg, M., and D. Schneider. 1994. Violence in American cities: Young black males is the answer, but what was the question? *Social Science and Medicine* 39(2):179-187.

Griffiths, E., C. Yule, and R. Gartner. 2011. Fighting over trivial things: Explaining the issue of contention in violent altercations. *Criminology* 49(1):61-94.

Grimes, T., J. Anderson, and L. Bergen. 2008. *Media Violence and Aggression: Science and Ideology*. Thousand Oaks, CA: Sage.

Grossman, D. C., B. A. Mueller, C. Riedy, M. D. Dowd, A. Villaveces, J. Prodzinski, J. Nakagawara, J. Howard, N. Thiersch, and R. Harruff. 2005. Gun storage practices and risk of youth suicide and unintentional firearm injuries. *Journal of the American Medical Association* 293(6):707-714.

Gunter, W. D., and K. Daly. 2012. Causal or spurious: Using propensity score matching to detangle the relationship between violent video games and violent behavior. *Computers in Human Behavior* 28(4):1348-1355.

Haddon, W., Jr. 1967. The prevention of accidents. In *Preventive Medicine*, edited by D. W. Clark and B. MacMahon. Boston, MA: Little, Brown. Pp. 591-621.

Haddon, W., Jr. 1968. The changing approach to the epidemiology, prevention, and amelioration of trauma: The transition to approaches etiologically rather than descriptively based. *American Journal of Public Health* 58(8):1431-1438.

Haddon, W., Jr. 1980. Options for the prevention of motor vehicle crash injury. *Israel Journal of Medical Sciences* 16(1):45-65.

Hahn, R. A., O. Bilukha, A. Crosby, M. T. Fullilove, A. Liberman, E. Moscicki, S. Snyder, F. Tuma, and P. A. Briss. 2005. Firearms laws and the reduction of violence: A systematic review. *American Journal of Preventive Medicine* 28(2 Suppl 1):40-71.

Hall, J. E., T. R. Simon, J. A. Mercy, R. Loeber, D. P. Farrington, and R. D. Lee. 2012. Centers for Disease Control and Prevention's Expert Panel on Protective Factors for Youth Violence Perpetration: Background and overview. *American Journal of Preventive Medicine* 43(2 Suppl 1):S1-S7.

HarassMap. 2013. *HarassMap: The blog.* http://blog.harassmap.org (accessed April 30, 2013).

Harlow, C. W. 2001. *Survey of inmates in state and federal correctional facilities: Firearm use by offenders, NCJ 189369.* Washington, DC: Bureau of Justice Statistics. http://www.bjs.gov/content/pub/pdf/fuo.pdf (accessed April 29, 2013).

Hemenway, D. 2001. The public health approach to motor vehicles, tobacco, and alcohol, with applications to firearms policy. *Journal of Public Health Policy* 22(4):381-402.

Hemenway, D., and M. Miller. 2013. Public health approach to the prevention of gun violence. *New England Journal of Medicine.* [Epub ahead of print]. http://www.nejm.org/doi/full/10.1056/NEJMsb1302631 (accessed May 8, 2013).

Hemenway, D., T. Shinoda-Tagawa, and M. Miller. 2002. Firearm availability and female homicide victimization rates among 25 populous high-income countries. *Journal of the American Medical Women's Association* 57(2):100-104.

Hemenway, D., C. Barber, and M. Miller. 2010. Unintentional firearm deaths: A comparison of other-inflicted and self-inflicted shootings. *Accident Analysis and Prevention* 42(4):1184-1188.

Hepburn, L., M. Miller, D. Azrael, and D. Hemenway. 2007. The US gun stock: Results from the 2004 national firearms survey. *Injury Prevention* 13(1):15-19.

Heron, M. 2012. Deaths: Leading causes for 2009. *National Vital Statistics Report* 61(7):1-96.

HHS and DOJ (U.S. Department of Health and Human Services and U.S. Department of Justice). 1996. *Surgeon General's Workshop on Violence and Public Health: Report,* HHS Publication No. HRS-D-MC 86-1. Washington, DC: Health Resources and Services Administration. http://profiles.nlm.nih.gov/ps/access/NNBCFX.pdf (accessed May 6, 2013).

Hindelang, M. J., M. R. Gottfredson, and J. Garofalo. 1978. *Victims of Personal Crime: An Empirical Foundation for a Theory of Personal Victimization.* Cambridge, MA: Ballinger.

Hirsch, J. K. 2006. A review of the literature on rural suicide: Risk and protective factors, incidence, and prevention. *Crisis* 27(4):189-199.

Hopf, W. H., G. L. Huber, and R. H. Weiß. 2008. Media violence and youth violence: A 2-year longitudinal study. *Journal of Media Psychology* 20(3):79-96.

Howard, G., R. T. Anderson, G. Russell, V. J. Howard, and G. L. Burke. 2000. Race, socioeconomic status, and cause-specific mortality. *Annals of Epidemiology* 10(4):214-223.

Hoyert, D. L., and J. Xu. 2012. Deaths: Preliminary data for 2011. *National Vital Statistics Reports* (6). http://www.cdc.gov/nchs/data/nvsr/nvsr61/nvsr61 _06.pdf (accessed April 15, 2013).

Huesmann, L. R. 1986. Psychological processes promoting the relation between exposure to media violence and aggressive behavior by the viewer. *Journal of Social Issues* 423:125-139.

Huesmann, L. R. 2007. The impact of electronic media violence: Scientific theory and research. *Journal of Adolescent Health* 41(6 Suppl 1):S6-S13.

Huesmann, L. R., and L. S. Miller. 1994. Long-term effects of repeated exposure to media violence in childhood. In *Aggressive Behavior: Current Perspectives*, edited by L. R. Huesmann. New York: Plenum Press. Pp. 153-186.

Huesmann, L. R., and L. D. Taylor. 2006. The role of media violence in violent behavior. *Annual Review of Public Health* 27:393-415.

Huesmann, L. R., K. Lagerspetz, and L. D. Eron. 1984. Intervening variables in the TV violence-aggression relation: Evidence from two countries. *Developmental Psychology* 20(5):746-775.

Huesmann, L. R., C. A. Anderson, L. Berkowitz, E. Donnerstein, J. D. Johnson, D. Linz, N. M. Malamuth, and E. Wartella. 2000. *Media violence influences on youth: Expert panel report to the U.S. Surgeon General.* Unpublished manuscript. Ann Arbor: University of Michigan Institute for Social Research.

Huesmann, L. R., J. Moise-Titus, C. L. Podolski, and L. D. Eron. 2003. Longitudinal relations between children's exposure to TV violence and their aggressive and violent behavior in young adulthood: 1977-1992. *Developmental Psychology* 39(2):201-221.

IOM (Institute of Medicine). 1999. *Reducing the Burden of Injury: Advancing Prevention and Treatment.* Washington, DC: National Academy Press.

IOM. 2008. *Violence Prevention in Low- and Middle-Income Countries: Finding a Place on the Global Agenda: Workshop Summary.* Washington, DC: The National Academies Press.

IOM. 2012. *Social and Economic Costs of Violence: Workshop Summary.* Washington, DC: The National Academies Press.

IOM. 2013. *Contagion of Violence: Workshop Summary.* Washington, DC: The National Academies Press.

Jackman, G. A., M. M. Farah, A. L. Kellermann, and H. K. Simon. 2001. Seeing is believing: What do boys do when they find a real gun? *Pediatrics* 107(6):1247-1250.

Jain, S., S. Gupta, and R. K. Thenua. 2012. A review on advancements in biometrics. *International Journal of Electronics and Computer Science Engineering* (3). http://www.ijecse.org/wp-content/uploads/2012/08/Volume-1Number-3PP-853-859.pdf (accessed April 10, 2013).

Jaiswal, S., S. S. Bhadauria, and R. S. Jadon. 2011. Biometric: Case study. *Journal of Global Research in Computer Science* (10). http://www.jgrcs.info/index.php/jgrcs/article/view/236 (accessed April 10, 2013).

Jennings, W. G., G. E. Higgins, R. Tewksbury, A. R. Gover, and A. R. Piquero. 2010. A longitudinal assessment of the victim-offender overlap. *Journal of Interpersonal Violence* 25(12):2147-2174.

Jensen, G. F., and D. Brownfield. 1986. Gender, lifestyles, and victimization: Beyond routine activity. *Violence and Victims* 1(2):85-99.

Johnson, R. M., M. Miller, M. Vriniotis, D. Azrael, and D. Hemenway. 2006. Are household firearms stored less safely in homes with adolescents? Analysis of a national random sample of parents. *Archives of Pediatrics & Adolescent Medicine* 160(8):788-792.

Kaiser Family Foundation. 2010. *Daily media use among children and teens up dramatically from five years ago.* http://kff.org/disparities-policy/press-release/daily-media-use-among-children-and-teens-up-dramatically-from-five years-ago (accessed May 8, 2013).

Kaplan, M. S., B. H. McFarland, and N. Huguet. 2009. Characteristics of adult male and female firearm suicide decedents: Findings from the National Violent Death Reporting System. *Injury Prevention* 15(5):322-327.

Karch, D. L., J. Logan, and N. Patel. 2011. Surveillance for violent deaths—National Violent Death Reporting System, 16 states, 2008. *Morbidity and Mortality Weekly Report* (SS10). http://www.cdc.gov/mmwr/preview/mm wrhtml/ss6010a1.htm (accessed April 29, 2013).

Karp, A. 2007. Completing the count: Civilian firearms. In *Small Arms Survey, 2007: Guns and the City.* Cambridge, UK: Cambridge University Press. Pp. 39-72.

Kellermann, A. L., and F. P. Rivara. 2013. Silencing the science on gun research. *Journal of the American Medical Association* 309(6):549-550.

Kellermann, A. L., R. K. Lee, and J. A. Mercy. 1991. The epidemiologic basis for the prevention of firearm injuries. *Annual Review of Public Health* 12:17-40.

Kellermann, A. L., F. P. Rivara, G. Somes, D. T. Reay, J. Francisco, J. G. Banton, J. Prodzinski, C. Fligner, and B. B. Hackman. 1992. Suicide in the home in relation to gun ownership. *New England Journal of Medicine* 327(7):467-472.

Kellermann, A. L., F. P. Rivara, N. B. Rushforth, J. G. Banton, D. T. Reay, J. T. Francisco, A. B. Locci, J. Prodzinski, B. B. Hackman, and G. Somes. 1993. Gun ownership as a risk factor for homicide in the home. *New England Journal of Medicine* 329(15):1084-1091.

Kellermann, A. L., L. Westphal, L. Fischer, and B. Harvard. 1995. Weapon involvement in home invasion crimes. *Journal of the American Medical Association* 273(22):1759-1762.

Kennedy, B. P., I. Kawachi, D. Prothrow-Stith, K. Lochner, and V. Gupta. 1998. Social capital, income inequality, and firearm violent crime. *Social Science and Medicine* 47(1):7-17.

Kennedy, D. M., A. M. Piehl, and A. A. Braga. 1996. Youth violence in Boston: Gun markets, serious youth offenders, and a use-reduction strategy. *Law and Contemporary Problems* 59(1):147-196.

Kleck, G. 1984. Handgun-only gun control: A policy disaster in the making. In *Firearms and Violence: Issues of Regulation*, edited by D. B. Kates. Cambridge, MA: Ballinger. Pp. 167-199.

Kleck, G. 1988. Crime-control through the private use of armed force. *Social Problems* 35(1):1-21.

Kleck, G. 1991. *Point Blank: Guns and Violence in America*. Hawthorne, NY: Aldine de Gruyter.

Kleck, G. 2001a. The frequency of defensive gun use: Evidence and disinformation. In *Armed: New Perspectives on Gun Control*, edited by G. Kleck and D. B. Kates. Amherst, NY: Prometheus Books. Pp. 213-284.

Kleck, G. 2001b. The nature and effectiveness of owning, carrying and using guns for self-protection. In *Armed: New Perspectives on Gun Control*, edited by G. Kleck and D. B. Kates. Amherst, NY: Prometheus Books. Pp. 285-342.

Kleck, G., and M. DeLone. 1993. Victim resistance and offender weapon effects in robbery. *Journal of Quantitative Criminology* 9(1):55-81.

Kleck, G., and M. Gertz. 1995. Armed resistance to crime: The prevalence and nature of self-defense with a gun. *Journal of Criminal Law & Criminology* 86(1):150-187.

Kleck, G., and E. B. Patterson. 1993. The impact of gun control and gun ownership levels on violence rates. *Journal of Quantitative Criminology* 9:249-287.

Kleck, G., and S.-Y. K. Wang. 2009. The myth of big-time gun trafficking and the overinterpretation of gun tracing data. *UCLA Law Review* (5). http://www.uclalawreview.org/pdf/56-5-6.pdf (accessed April 29, 2013).

Kochanek, K. D., J. Xu, S. L. Murphy, A. M. Minino, and H. C. Kung. 2011. Deaths: Final data for 2009. *National Vital Statistics Report* (3). http://www.cdc.gov/nchs/data/nvsr/nvsr60/nvsr60_03.pdf (accessed April 29, 2013).

Krahé, B., and I. Möller. 2010. Longitudinal effects of media violence on aggression and empathy among German adolescents. *Journal of Applied Developmental Psychology* 31(5):401-409.

Krahé, B., I. Möller, L. R. Huesmann, L. Kirwil, J. Felber, and A. Berger. 2011. Desensitization to media violence: Links with habitual media violence exposure, aggressive cognitions, and aggressive behavior. *Journal of Personality and Social Psychology* 100(4):630-646.

Krouse, W. J. 2012. *Gun control legislation*. Washington, DC: Congressional Research Service. http://www.fas.org/sgp/crs/misc/RL32842.pdf (accessed April 29, 2013).

Kuhn, E. M., C. L. Nie, M. E. O'Brien, R. L. Withers, G. J. Wintemute, and S. W. Hargarten. 2002. Missing the target: A comparison of buyback and fatality related guns. *Injury Prevention* 8(2):143-146.

Kung, H. C., J. L. Pearson, and X. Liu. 2003. Risk factors for male and female suicide decedents ages 15-64 in the United States—results from the 1993 National Mortality Followback Survey. *Social Psychiatry and Psychiatric Epidemiology* 38(8):419-426.

Kutner, L., and C. Olson. 2008. *Grand Theft Childhood: The Surprising Truth About Violent Video Games and What Parents Can Do*. New York: Simon & Schuster.

Langton, L. 2012. *Firearms stolen during household burglaries and other property crimes, 2005-2010, NCJ 239436*. Washington, DC: Bureau of Justice Statistics. http://bjs.gov/content/pub/pdf/fshbopc0510.pdf (accessed April 29, 2013).

Law Center to Prevent Gun Violence. 2013. *Statistics on gun deaths & injuries*. http://smartgunlaws.org/gun-deaths-and-injuries-statistics (accessed April 8, 2013).

Lenhart, A., J. Kahne, E. Middaugh, A. R. Macgill, C. Evans, and J. Vitak. 2008. *Teens, video games, and civics*. Washington, DC: Pew Internet & American Life Project. http://www.pewinternet.org/Reports/2008/Teens-Video-Games-and-Civics.aspx (accessed May 8, 2013).

Makarios, M. D., and T. C. Pratt. 2012. The effectiveness of policies and programs that attempt to reduce firearm violence: A meta-analysis. *Crime & Delinquency* 58(2):222-244.

Markovic, J. 2012. Criminal justice and public health approaches to violent crime: Complementary perspectives. *Geography and Public Safety* (2). http://cops.usdoj.gov/Publications/e05122469c.pdf (accessed April 8, 2013).

Marvell, T. B., and C. E. Moody. 1995. The impact of enhanced prison terms for felonies committed with guns. *Criminology* 33(2):247-281.

Massachusetts Executive Office of Health and Human Services. 2013. *Weapon Related Injury Surveillance Systems (WRISS)*. http://www.mass.gov/eohhs/gov/departments/dph/programs/health-stats/injury-surveillance/reports/weapon-related-injury-surveillance-system.html (accessed April 17, 2013).

McDowall, D., C. Loftin, and B. Wiersema. 1992. A comparative study of the preventive effects of mandatory sentencing laws for gun crimes. *Journal of Criminal Law & Criminology* 83(2):378-394.

McDowall, D., C. Loftin, and B. Wiersema. 1998. Estimates of the frequency of firearm self-defense from the redesigned National Crime Victimization Survey. *Violence Research Group Discussion Paper 20*. College Park, MD: University of Maryland Department of Criminology and Criminal Justice.

McIntyre, J. J., Jr., Teevan, J. J., and T. Hartnagel. 1972. Television violence and deviant behavior. In *Television and Social Behavior: Vol. 3, Television and Adolescent Aggressiveness*, edited by G. A. Comstock and E. A. Rubenstein. Washington, DC: U.S. Government Printing Office. Pp. 383-435.

Milavsky, J. R., R. C. Kessler, H. H. Stipp, and W. S. Rubens. 1982. *Television and Aggression: A Panel Study*. New York: Academic Press.

Miller, M., D. Azrael, and D. Hemenway. 2001. Firearm availability and unintentional firearm deaths. *Accident Analysis and Prevention* 33(4):477-484.

Miller, T. R. 2010. *Societal cost per firearm injury, United States, 2010*. Calverton, MD: Pacific Institute for Research and Evaluation. http://www.pire.org/documents/GSWcost2010.pdf (accessed April 29, 2013).

Mozaffarian, D., A. Afshin, N. L. Benowitz, V. Bittner, S. R. Daniels, H. A. Franch, D. R. Jacobs, W. E. Kraus, P. M. Kris-Etherton, D. A. Krummel, B. M. Popkin, L. P. Whitsel, and N. A. Zakai. 2012. Population approaches to improve diet, physical activity, and smoking habits: A scientific statement from the American Heart Association. *Circulation* 126(12):1514-1563.

Mozaffarian, D., D. Hemenway, and D. S. Ludwig. 2013. Curbing gun violence: Lessons from public health successes. *Journal of the American Medical Association* 309(6):551-552.

NAE (National Academy of Engineering). 2003. *Owner-Authorized Handguns*. Washington, DC: The National Academies Press.

NAE. 2005. *Technological Options for User-Authorized Handguns: A Technology-Readiness Assessment*. Washington, DC: The National Academies Press.

Nance, M. L., L. Denysenko, D. R. Durbin, C. C. Branas, P. W. Stafford, and C. Schwab. 2002. The rural-urban continuum: Variability in statewide serious firearm injuries in children and adolescents. *Archives of Pediatrics & Adolescent Medicine* 156(8):781-785.

NCHS (National Center for Health Statistics). 2012. *LCWK1. Deaths, percent of total deaths, and death rates for the 15 leading causes of death in 5-year age groups, by race and sex: United States, 2010*. http://www.cdc.gov/nchs/data/dvs/LCWK1_2010.pdf (accessed April 29, 2013).

Newcombe, T. 2013. *Transparency, social media and gun safety*. http://www.governing.com/columns/col-transparency-social-media-gun-safety.html (accessed April 10, 2013).

Nielsen, A. L., and R. Martinez. 2003. Reassessing the alcohol-violence linkage: Results from a multiethnic city. *Justice Quarterly* 20(3):445-469.

NIJ (National Institute of Justice). 2008. *Gun violence program: Operation Ceasefire.* http://www.nij.gov/topics/crime/gun-violence/prevention/ceasefire. htm (accessed April 30, 2013).

NRC (National Research Council). 2005. *Firearms and Violence: A Critical Review.* Washington, DC: The National Academies Press.

NRC and IOM. 1985. *Injury in America: A Continuing Public Health Problem.* Washington, DC: National Academy Press.

O'Keefe, G. S. 1984. Public views on crime: Television exposure and media credibility. In *Communication Yearbook 8,* edited by R. N. Bostrom. Beverly Hills, CA: Sage. Pp. 514-535.

Olson, C. K., L. A. Kutner, L. Baer, E. V. Beresin, D. E. Warner, and A. M. Nicholi II. 2009. M-rated video games and aggressive or problem behavior among young adolescents. *Applied Developmental Science* 13(4):188-198.

Onwuachi-Saunders, C., and D. F. Hawkins. 1993. Black-white differences in injury. Race or social class? *Annals of Epidemiology* 3(2):150-153.

Osgood, D. W., J. K. Wilson, P. M. O'Malley, J. G. Bachman, and L. D. Johnston. 1996. Routine activities and individual deviant behavior. *American Sociological Review* 61(4):635-655.

Otto, M. W., A. Henin, D. R. Hirshfeld-Becker, M. H. Pollack, J. Biederman, and J. F. Rosenbaum. 2007. Posttraumatic stress disorder symptoms following media exposure to tragic events: Impact of 9/11 on children at risk for anxiety disorders. *Journal of Anxiety Disorders* 21(7):888-902.

Paik, H., and G. Comstock. 1994. The effects of television violence on antisocial behavior: A meta-analysis. *Communication Research* 21(4):516-546.

Papachristos, A. V. 2009. Murder by structure: Dominance relations and the social structure of gang homicide. *American Journal of Sociology* 115(1): 74-128.

PatentStorm, LLC. 2013. *PatentStorm.* www.patentstorm.us (accessed April 10, 2013).

Pew Research Center. 2013. *Why own a gun? Protection is now top reason.* http://www.people-press.org/2013/03/12/why-own-a-gun-protection-is-now top-reason (accessed April 29, 2013).

Phillips, D. P. 1982. The impact of fictional television stories on U.S. adult fatalities: New evidence on the effect of the mass media on violence. *American Journal of Sociology* 87(6):1340-1359.

Pirkis, J. E., P. M. Burgess, C. Francis, R. W. Blood, and D. J. Jolley. 2006. The relationship between media reporting of suicide and actual suicide in Australia. *Social Science & Medicine* 62(11):2874-2886.

Przybylski, A. K., C. S. Rigby, and R. M. Ryan. 2010. A motivational model of video game engagement. *Review of General Psychology* 14(2):154-166.

Reeves, A., D. Stuckler, M. McKee, D. Gunnell, S. S. Chang, and S. Basu. 2012. Increase in state suicide rates in the USA during economic recession. *Lancet* 380(9856):1813-1814.

Richardson, E. G., and D. Hemenway. 2011. Homicide, suicide, and unintentional firearm fatality: Comparing the United States with other high-income countries, 2003. *Journal of Trauma* 70(1):238-243.

Robinson, J. P., and J. G. Bachman. 1972. Television viewing habits and aggression. In *Television and Social Behavior: Vol. 3, Television and Adolescent Aggressiveness*, edited by G. A. Comstock and E. A. Rubenstein. Washington, DC: U.S. Government Printing Office. Pp. 372-382.

Ross, C. E., and J. Mirowsky. 2001. Neighborhood disadvantage, disorder, and health. *Journal of Health and Social Behavior* 42(3):258-276.

Rossow, I., and T. Norstrom. 2012. The impact of small changes in bar closing hours on violence. The Norwegian experience from 18 cities. *Addiction* 107(3):530-537.

Rubinstein, E. A. 1983. Television and behavior. Research conclusions of the 1982 NIMH report and their policy implications. *The American Psychologist* 38(7):820-825.

Ruddell, R., and G. L. Mays. 2004. Risky behavior, juveniles, guns, and unintentional firearms fatalities. *Youth Violence and Juvenile Justice* 2(4):342-358.

Runyan, C. W. 1998. Using the Haddon matrix: Introducing the third dimension. *Injury Prevention* 4(4):302-307.

Sampson, R. J., and J. L. Lauritsen. 1990. Deviant lifestyles, proximity to crime, and the offender-victim link in personal violence. *Journal of Research in Crime and Delinquency* 27(2):110-139.

Sampson, R. J., S. W. Raudenbush, and F. Earls. 1997. Neighborhoods and violent crime: A multilevel study of collective efficacy. *Science* 277 (5328):918-924.

Sampson, R. J., J. D. Morenoff, and S. Raudenbush. 2005. Social anatomy of racial and ethnic disparities in violence. *American Journal of Public Health* 95(2):224-232.

Satcher, D. 1995. Violence as a public health issue. *Bulletin of the New York Academy of Medicine* 72(1):46-56.

Savage, J. 2004. Does viewing violent media really cause criminal violence? A methodological review. *Aggression and Violent Behavior* 10(1):99-128.

Savage, J., and C. Yancey. 2008. The effects of media violence exposure on criminal aggression: A meta-analysis. *Criminal Justice and Behavior* 35(6):772-791.

Saylor, C. F., B. L. Cowart, J. A. Lipovsky, C. Jackson, and A. J. Finch, Jr. 2003. Media exposure to September 11: Elementary school students' experiences and posttraumatic symptoms. *American Behavioral Scientist* 46(12):1622-1642.

Scribner, R. A., D. P. MacKinnon, and J. H. Dwyer. 1995. The risk of assaultive violence and alcohol availability in Los Angeles County. *American Journal of Public Health* 85(3):335-340.

Sharkey, P. T., N. Tirado-Strayer, A. V. Papachristos, and C. C. Raver. 2012. The effect of local violence on children's attention and impulse control. *American Journal of Public Health* 102(12):2287-2293.

Sheley, J. F., and J. D. Wright. 1995. *In the line of fire: Youth, guns, and violence in urban America.* New York: Aldine de Gruyter.

Shepherd, J. P., I. Sutherland, and R. G. Newcombe. 2006. Relations between alcohol, violence and victimization in adolescence. *Journal of Adolescence* 29(4):539-553.

Simon, T. R., C. W. Dent, and S. Sussman. 1997. Vulnerability to victimization, concurrent problem behaviors, and peer influence as predictors of in-school weapon carrying among high school students. *Violence and Victims* 12:277-289.

Sims, D. W., B. A. Bivins, F. N. Obeid, H. M. Horst, V. J. Sorensen, and J. J. Fath. 1989. Urban trauma: A chronic recurrent disease. *Journal of Trauma* 29(7):940-947.

Sinauer, N., J. L. Annest, and J. A. Mercy. 1996. Unintentional, nonfatal firearm-related injuries—a preventable public health burden. *Journal of the American Medical Association* 275(22):1740-1743.

Singh, G. K., and M. Siahpush. 2002. Increasing rural-urban gradients in US suicide mortality, 1970-1997. *American Journal of Public Health* 92(7):1161-1167.

Skogan, W. G., S. M. Hartnett, N. Bump, and J. Dubois. 2008. *Evaluation of CeaseFire–Chicago.* Chicago, IL: U.S. Department of Justice. https://www.ncjrs.gov/pdffiles1/nij/grants/227181.pdf (accessed April 8, 2013).

Slater, M. D., K. L. Henry, R. C. Swaim, and L. L. Anderson. 2003. Violent media content and aggressiveness in adolescents: A downward spiral model. *Communication Research* 30(6):713-736.

Slovak, K., and K. Carlson. 2004. Firearms, violence, and attitudes among rural youth. *Journal of Rural Community Psychology* E7(1). http://muwww.new.marshall.edu/jrcp/E62_slovak.htm (accessed April 29, 2013).

Slovak, K., and M. Singer. 2001. Gun violence exposure and trauma among rural youth. *Violence and Victims* 16(4):389-400.

Sorenson, S. B. 2006. Firearm use in intimate partner violence: A brief overview. *Evaluation Review* 30(3):229-236.

Southwick, L. 2000. Self-defense with guns—the consequences. *Journal of Criminal Justice* 28(5):351-370.

Spano, R., C. Rivera, and J. M. Bolland. 2010. Are chronic exposure to violence and chronic violent behavior closely related developmental processes during adolescence? *Criminal Justice and Behavior* 37(10):1160-1179.

Spano, R., W. A. Pridemore, and J. Bolland. 2012. Specifying the role of exposure to violence and violent behavior on initiation of gun carrying: A longitudinal test of three models of youth gun carrying. *Journal of Interpersonal Violence* 27(1):158-176.

Sparks, C. S. 2011. Violent crime in San Antonio, Texas: An application of spatial epidemiological methods. *Spatial and Spatiotemporal Epidemiology* 2(4):301-309.

Sparks, R. F. 1982. *Research on Victims of Crime: Accomplishments, Issues, and New Directions*. Washington, DC: U.S. Department of Health and Human Services.

Stack, S. 2003. Media coverage as a risk factor in suicide. *Journal of Epidemiology & Community Health* 57(4):238-240.

Stack, S. 2005. Suicide in the media: A quantitative review of studies based on non-fictional stories. *Suicide and Life-Threatening Behavior* 35(2):121-133.

Sumner, S. A., P. M. Layde, and C. E. Guse. 2008. Firearm death rates and association with level of firearm purchase background check. *American Journal of Preventive Medicine* 35(1):1-6.

Surgeon General's Scientific Advisory Committee on Television and Social Behavior. 1972. *Television and Growing Up: The Impact of Televised Violence*. Report to the Surgeon General, U.S. Public Health Service. Rockville, MD: National Institute of Mental Health. http://profiles.nlm.nih.gov/NN/B/C/G/X (accessed May 8, 2013).

Tark, J., and G. Kleck. 2004. Resisting crime: The effects of victim action on the outcomes of crimes. *Criminology* 42(4):861-910.

Teret, S. 2013. *Technology Research Priorities*. Presented at the Institute of Medicine and National Research Council Workshop for the Committee on Priorities for a Public Health Research Agenda to Reduce the Threat of Firearm-Related Violence, Washington, DC, April 23.

Teret, S. P., and P. L. Culross. 2002. Product-oriented approaches to reducing youth gun violence. *Children, Youth, and Gun Violence* (2). http://futureofchildren.org/futureofchildren/publications/docs/12_02_08.pdf (accessed April 15, 2013).

Teret, S. P., S. DeFrancesco, S. W. Hargarten, and K. D. Robinson. 1998. Making guns safer. *Issues in Science and Technology*. http://www.issues.org/14.4/teret.htm (accessed April 10, 2013).

Tousignant, M., B. L. Mishara, A. Caillaud, V. Fortin, and D. St-Laurent. 2005. The impact of media coverage of the suicide of a well-known Quebec reporter: The case of Gaetan Girouard. *Social Science & Medicine* 60(9):1919-1926.

Truman, J. L. 2011. *National Crime Victimization Survey—criminal victimization, 2010, NCJ 235508*. Washington, DC: Bureau of Justice Statistics. http://bjs.gov/content/pub/pdf/cv10.pdf (accessed April 15, 2013).

Truman, J. L., and M. R. Rand. 2010. *National Crime Victimization Survey—criminal victimization, 2009, NCJ 231327*. Washington, DC: Bureau of Justice Statistics. http://bjs.gov/content/pub/pdf/cv09.pdf (accessed April 8, 2013).

U.S. Census Bureau. 2012. *Table 310. Murder victims—circumstances and weapons used or cause of death: 2000 to 2009*. http://www.census.gov/compendia/statab/2012/tables/12s0310.pdf (accessed April 17, 2013).

Valenta, C. R., D. McGuinness, and J. Dowling. 2013. *RFID firearm safety mechanism*. http://www.georgiatech.ie/?publication=rfid-firearm-safety-mechanism&wppa_open=1 (accessed April 10, 2013).

Vigdor, E. R., and J. A. Mercy. 2006. Do laws restricting access to firearms by domestic violence offenders prevent intimate partner homicide? *Evaluation Review* 30(3):313-346.

Webster, D. W., P. S. Gainer, and H. R. Champion. 1993. Weapon carrying among inner-city junior high school students: Defensive behavior vs. aggressive delinquency. *American Journal of Public Health* 83(11):1604-1608.

Weiner, J., D. J. Wiebe, T. S. Richmond, K. Beam, A. L. Berman, C. C. Branas, R. A. Cheney, T. Coyne-Beasley, J. Firman, M. Fishbein, S. Hargarten, D. Hemenway, R. Jeffcoat, D. Kennedy, C. S. Koper, J. Lemaire, M. Miller, J. A. Roth, C. W. Schwab, R. Spitzer, S. Teret, J. Vernick, and D. Webster. 2007. Reducing firearm violence: A research agenda. *Injury Prevention* 13(2):80-84.

Weiss, D. R. 1996. *Smart Gun Technology Project final report*. Paper submitted by Sandia National Laboratories to the U.S. Department of Energy, Washington, DC. http://prod.sandia.gov/techlib/access-control.cgi/1996/961131.pdf (accessed April 10, 2013).

White House. 2013a. *Now is the time: The President's plan to protect our children and our communities by reducing gun violence*. http://www.whitehouse.gov/sites/default/files/docs/wh_now_is_the_time_full.time_full.pdf (accessed April 8, 2013).

White House. 2013b. *Presidential memorandum—engaging in public health research on the causes and prevention of gun violence*. http://www.whitehouse.gov/the-press-office/2013/01/16/presidential-memorandum-engaging-public-health-research-causes-and-preve (accessed April 8, 2013).

WHO (World Health Organization). 2002. *World Report on Violence and Health*, edited by E. G. Krug, L. L. Dahlberg, J. A. Mercy, A. B. Zwi, and R. Lozano. Geneva: WHO. http://www.who.int/violence_injury_prevention/violence/world_report/en (accessed April 7, 2013).

Wilson, D. K., W. Kliewer, and D. A. Sica. 2004. The relationship between exposure to violence and blood pressure mechanisms. *Current Hypertension Reports* 6(4):321-326.

Wilson, J. Q., and G. L. Kelling. 1982. Broken windows: The police and neighborhood safety. *Atlantic Monthly* (March):29-38, http://www.the atlantic.com/magazine/archive/1982/03/broken-windows/304465 (accessed May 15, 2013).

Wintemute, G. 2010. Firearm retailers' willingness to participate in an illegal gun purchase. *Journal of Urban Health* 87(5):865-878.

Wintemute, G. J., P. Cook, and M. Wright. 2005. Risk factors among handgun retailers for frequent and disproportionate sales of guns used in violent and firearm related crimes. *Injury Prevention* 11(6):357-363.

Wirsbinski, J. W. 2001. "Smart gun" technology. Paper submitted by Sandia National Laboratories to the U.S. Department of Energy. http://prod. sandia.gov/techlib/access-control.cgi/2001/013499.pdf (accessed April 10, 2013).

Wood, W., F. Y. Wong, and J. Gregory Chachere. 1991. Effects of media violence on viewers' aggression in unconstrained social interaction. *Psychological Bulletin* 109(3):371-383.

Wright, J. D., and P. H. Rossi. 1986. *Armed and Considered Dangerous: A Survey of Felons and Their Firearms*. New York: Aldine de Gruyter.

Wright, R. J., and S. F. Steinbach. 2001. Violence: An unrecognized environmental exposure that may contribute to greater asthma morbidity in high risk inner-city populations. *Environmental Health Perspectives* 109(10): 1085-1089.

Ybarra, M. L., M. Diener-West, D. Markow, P. J. Leaf, M. Hamburger, and P. Boxer. 2008. Linkages between internet and other media violence with seriously violent behavior by youth. *Pediatrics* 122(5):929-937.

Ylikoski, M. E. 1995. Self-reported elevated blood pressure in army officers with hearing loss and gunfire noise exposure. *Military Medicine* 160(8): 388-390.

Zawitz, M. W. 1995. *Firearms, crime, and criminal justice: Guns used in crime, NCJ-148201*. Washington, DC: U.S. Department of Justice. http://bjs. gov/content/pub/pdf/GUIC.PDF (accessed April 10, 2013).

Zeoli, A. M., and D. W. Webster. 2010. Effects of domestic violence policies, alcohol taxes, and police staffing levels on intimate partner homicide in large U.S. cities. *Injury Prevention* 16(2):90-95.

Zimmerman, G. M., and S. F. Messner. 2013. Individual, family background, and contextual explanations of racial and ethnic disparities in youths' exposure to violence. *American Journal of Public Health* 103(3):435-442.

Zona, K., and S. Milan. 2011. Gender differences in the longitudinal impact of exposure to violence on mental health in urban youth. *Journal of Youth and Adolescence* 40(12):1674-1690.

B

Public Meeting and Workshop Agenda

Monday, April 22, 2013
Room 201

National Academies Keck Center
500 Fifth Street, NW
Keck Building
Washington, DC 20001

OPEN SESSION

BACKGROUND AND OVERVIEW

Session objectives: To obtain a better understanding of the background to the study and the charge to the committee. To have a discussion with the study sponsor about what a public health agenda should and should not include. To consider a process for prioritizing a research agenda.

3:30 p.m.   Welcome and Introductions

ALAN LESHNER, *Committee Chair*
Chief Executive Officer
American Association for the Advancement of Science
   (AAAS)
Executive Publisher, *Science*

3:45 p.m.   Background and Charge to the Committee
                   LINDA DEGUTIS
                   Director
                   National Center for Injury Prevention and Control
                   Centers for Disease Control and Prevention (CDC)

4:15 p.m.   Committee Discussion with Sponsor

5:00 p.m.   Panel Discussion: Strategies and Criteria to Prioritize a
                   Research Agenda

                   DAVID FLEMING
                   Director
                   Seattle–King County Health Department

                   DEAN JAMISON
                   Professor, Global Health
                   Adjunct Professor, Health Services
                   Department of Global Health
                   University of Washington

5:30 p.m.   Committee Discussion with Panelists

6:00 p.m.   Adjourn

Tuesday, April 23, 2013
Room 100

National Academies Keck Center
500 Fifth Street, NW
Washington, DC 20001

Background:

Firearms are often a factor in both self-directed and interpersonal violence-
related deaths and injuries, and understanding more about the relationship between firearms and violence is essential to improving population health and
safety. Critical information is needed to improve our understanding of how best
to prevent firearm-related violence and its consequences, including

- Conducting research to identify risks and protective factors for gun violence to guide effective prevention strategies.
- Evaluating the effectiveness of interventions to prevent gun-related violence, including those likely to have the greatest public health impact.

This workshop will invite stakeholders to provide input on potential themes of a research agenda that will examine how to prevent gun violence, including firearm homicides, suicides, and nonfatal injuries, the interventions and prevention strategies that are currently used and that need to be evaluated as well as new and innovative strategies, and the variety of risk and protective factors associated with firearms. The proposed agenda should identify research questions that can be answered in the short term that can lead to the greatest public health impact and research questions that can shed light on the characteristics of gun violence and the potential to prevent gun violence.

Meeting Objectives:

The workshop will seek to explore potential research topics in the following five areas: (1) characteristics of gun violence, (2) interventions and strategies, (3) technology, (4) video games and other media, and (5) risk and protective factors. Identified research topics should be those that can be answered in the short term and those that can lead to the greatest public health impact.

OPEN SESSION

8:30 a.m.   Welcoming Remarks

JUDITH SALERNO
Leonard D. Schaeffer Executive Officer
Institute of Medicine

ROBERT HAUSER
Executive Director
Division of Behavioral and Social Sciences and Education
National Research Council

8:35 a.m.   Committee Introductions and Meeting Objectives

ALAN LESHNER, *Committee Chair*
Chief Executive Officer, AAAS
Executive Publisher, *Science*

8:45 a.m.   Context for and Charge to the Committee

                   LINDA DEGUTIS
                   Director
                   National Center for Injury Prevention and Control
                   CDC

9:00 a.m.   Discussion with the Committee

SESSION I: DATA GAPS IN POLICY DISCUSSIONS

Session objective: Identify data and evidence-based research needs that may inform ongoing and future policy discussions as they relate to gun-related violence and prevention.

9:15 a.m.   Session Objectives

                   ALAN LESHNER, *Committee Chair*
                   Chief Executive Officer, AAAS
                   Executive Publisher, *Science*

9:20 a.m.   Panel Discussion: What Research Is Needed to Help to
                   Inform Policy

                   RICHARD FELDMAN
                   President
                   Independent Firearm Owners Association

                   PHILIP COOK
                   Senior Associate Dean for Faculty and Research
                   ITT/Terry Sanford Professor of Public Policy
                   Professor of Economics and Sociology and Faculty
                       Affiliate, Center for Child and Family Policy
                   Duke Sanford School of Public Policy

                   DANIEL GROSS
                   President
                   Brady Campaign to Prevent Gun Violence

KEITH HOTLE
Chronic Disease and Substance Abuse Unit Manager
Suicide Prevention Team Leader
Public Health Division, Wyoming Department of
Health

JOHN FRAZER
Director
Research and Information Division
National Rifle Association Institute for Legislative Action

10:20 a.m.   Discussion with Committee

ALAN LESHNER, *Committee Chair*
Chief Executive Officer, AAAS
Executive Publisher, *Science*

11:00 a.m.   BREAK

SESSION II: OVERVIEW OF ONGOING VIOLENCE RESEARCH

Session objectives: Review currently funded research topics for gun-related violence and prevention. Explore relevant key areas of research currently being conducted on non-gun-related violence and prevention.

11:15 a.m.   Panel Discussion: Gun Violence and Prevention Research
Activities

STEPHEN HARGARTEN, *Moderator*
Professor and Chair
Department of Emergency Medicine
Director, Injury Research Center
Associate Dean, Global Health
Medical College of Wisconsin

NINA VINIK
Program Director
Gun Violence Prevention
The Joyce Foundation

DANIEL WEBSTER
Center for Gun Policy and Research
Johns Hopkins Bloomberg School of Public Health

GREG RIDGEWAY
Director
National Institute of Justice

PAUL BLACKMAN
Research Coordinator (Retired)
National Rifle Association

12:15 p.m.   Discussion with Committee

STEPHEN HARGARTEN, *Moderator*
Professor and Chair
Department of Emergency Medicine
Director, Injury Research Center
Associate Dean, Global Health
Medical College of Wisconsin

12:45 p.m.   Lunch

1:30 p.m.   Panel Discussion: Ongoing Non-Gun-Related Violence
and Prevention Research

STEPHEN HARGARTEN, *Moderator*
Professor and Chair
Department of Emergency Medicine
Director, Injury Research Center
Associate Dean, Global Health
Medical College of Wisconsin

JULIA DA SILVA
Director, Violence Prevention Office
American Psychological Association

DEBORAH GORMAN-SMITH
Professor
University of Chicago School of Social Service
    Administration

MATTHEW MILLER
Associate Director, Harvard Injury Control Research
    Center
Associate Professor, Department of Health Policy
    and Management
Harvard University

JACQUELYN CAMPBELL
Professor and Anna D. Wolf Chair
Department of Community-Public Health
School of Nursing, Johns Hopkins University

2:30 p.m.   Discussion with Committee

STEPHEN HARGARTEN, *Moderator*
Professor and Chair
Department of Emergency Medicine
Director, Injury Research Center
Associate Dean, Global Health
Medical College of Wisconsin

SESSION III: PUBLIC COMMENT

Session objective: Seek public comment from interested stakeholders about key research topics for a public health research agenda that would assess the causes of gun violence and evaluate existing or potential public health interventions to prevent firearm-related violence.

Note: To accommodate requests, speakers will be strictly limited to 3 minutes.

3:00 p.m.   Public Comment: Topics for a Public Health Research
                   Agenda on Gun Violence

ALAN LESHNER, *Committee Chair*
Chief Executive Officer, AAAS
Executive Publisher, *Science*

SESSION IV: RESEARCH PRIORITIES: BREAKOUT SESSIONS

Session objectives: Identify key public health research that would assess the causes of gun violence and evaluate existing or potential public health interventions to prevent firearm-related violence. Provide an evidence base for why that research is needed.

3:30 p.m.   Session Objectives

ALAN LESHNER, *Committee Chair*
Chief Executive Officer, AAAS
Executive Publisher, *Science*

3:45-6:00 p.m.   Breakout Panels
                       A (Room 100)
                       B (Room 204)
                       C (Room 202)
                       D (Room 206)
                       E (Room 110)

BREAKOUT A: CHARACTERISTICS OF GUN VIOLENCE

Breakout objective: Identify research questions necessary to improve understanding of the characteristics of both fatal and nonfatal gun violence.

3:45 p.m.   Panel Discussion: Characteristics of Gun Violence

                       SUSAN SORENSON, *Moderator*
                       Professor of Social Policy
                       Senior Fellow in Public Health
                       University of Pennsylvania

                       JAY CORZINE
                       Professor of Sociology
                       University of Central Florida

                       SHELDON GREENBERG
                       Associate Dean of the School of Education
                       Division of Public Safety Leadership
                       Associate Professor of Management
                       Johns Hopkins University

                       DAVID HEMENWAY
                       Director
                       Injury Control Research Center
                       Harvard University

                       JON VERNICK
                       Associate Professor
                       Co-Director, Johns Hopkins Center for Gun Policy and
                           Research
                       Deputy Director, Johns Hopkins Center for Injury
                           Research and Policy
                       Johns Hopkins Bloomberg School of Public Health

5:00 p.m.   Discussion with Committee and Participants

                   SUSAN SORENSON, *Moderator*
                   Professor of Social Policy
                   Senior Fellow in Public Health
                   University of Pennsylvania

6:00 p.m.   Adjourn

BREAKOUT B: INTERVENTION RESEARCH PRIORITIES

Breakout objective: Identify research questions that are necessary to improve understanding of the effectiveness of interventions and strategies to prevent or reduce gun-related injuries. These may include, but should not be limited to, research questions related to the impact of public education campaigns, youth access to and use of guns, safe storage practices, access to guns, and improved personal protection.

3:45 p.m.   Panel Discussion: Intervention Research Priorities

                   JEFF RUNGE, *Moderator*
                   Principal
                   The Chertoff Group

                   ROSEANNA ANDER
                   Executive Director
                   University of Chicago Crime Lab

                   CHARLES BRANAS
                   Professor of Epidemiology
                   University of Pennsylvania Perelman School of Medicine

                   CARLISLE MOODY
                   Professor of Economics
                   The College of William and Mary

                   GAREN WINTEMUTE
                   Professor of Emergency Medicine
                   Director, Violence Prevention Research Program
                   University of California, Davis

5:00 p.m.   Discussion with Committee and Participants

                     JEFF RUNGE, *Moderator*
                     Principal
                     The Chertoff Group

6:00 p.m.   Adjourn

BREAKOUT C: TECHNOLOGY RESEARCH PRIORITIES

Breakout objective: Identify research questions related to potential technologies that may reduce gun-related violence, including how guns and ammunition can be designed and engineered to improve safety and prevent misuse.

3:45 p.m.   Panel Discussion: Technology Research Priorities

                     DONALD CARLUCCI, *Moderator*
                     Senior Research Scientist (ST)
                     U.S. Army Armament, Research, Development and
                         Engineering Center, Picatinny Arsenal

                     JOSEPH DOWLING
                     General Manager
                     Senior Researcher and Technical Lead
                     Georgia Tech Ireland

                     MARK GREENE
                     General Engineer
                     National Institute of Justice

                     DONALD SEBASTIAN
                     Senior Vice President for Research & Development
                     New Jersey Institute of Technology

                     STEPHEN TERET
                     Director, Center for Law and the Public's Health
                     Johns Hopkins Bloomberg School of Public Health

5:00 p.m.   Discussion with Committee and Participants

                     DONALD CARLUCCI, *Moderator*
                     Senior Research Scientist (ST)
                     U.S. Army Armament, Research, Development and
                         Engineering Center, Picatinny Arsenal

6:00 p.m.   Adjourn

BREAKOUT D: VIDEO GAMES AND OTHER MEDIA

Breakout objective: Identify questions that improve understanding of the impact of violence in video games, the media, and social media on real-life violence.

3:45 p.m.	Panel Discussion: Research Priorities to Understand the Impact of Video Games and Other Media

> RONALD KESSLER, *Moderator*
> McNeil Family Professor of Health Care Policy
> Harvard Medical School

> BRAD BUSHMAN
> Professor of Communication and Psychology
> Margaret Hall and Robert Randal Rinehart Chair of Mass
>   Communication
> School of Communication
> Ohio State University

> CHRISTOPHER FERGUSON
> Associate Professor
> Psychology and Criminal Justice
> Texas A&M International University

> NADINE KASLOW
> Professor and Vice Chair for Faculty Development
> Department of Psychiatry and Behavioral Sciences
> Emory University School of Medicine

> JOHN MURRAY
> Research Fellow, Department of Psychology
> Washington College
> Visiting Scholar, Center on Media and Child Health
> Children's Hospital Boston, Harvard Medical School

5:00 p.m.	Discussion with Committee and Participants

> RONALD KESSLER, *Moderator*
> McNeil Family Professor of Health Care Policy
> Harvard Medical School

6:00 p.m.	Adjourn

BREAKOUT E: RISK AND PROTECTIVE FACTORS RESEARCH PRIORITIES

Breakout objective: Identify research questions that will assess potential risk and protective factors and other critical issues, such as socioeconomic and socio-cultural environments.

3:45 p.m.   Panel Discussion: Risk and Protective Factors Research Priorities

JOHN RICH, *Moderator*
Professor and Chair of Health Management and Policy
Drexel University School of Public Health

JAMES GILLIGAN
Clinical Professor of Psychiatry
New York University School of Medicine

ARTHUR KELLERMANN
Paul O'Neill-Alcoa Chair in Policy Analysis
RAND Health
RAND Corporation

SHARON LAMBERT
Associate Professor of Clinical and Community Psychology
Department of Psychology
The George Washington University

DEANNA WILKINSON
Associate Professor
Department of Human Development & Family Science
The Ohio State University

5:00 p.m.   Discussion with Committee and Participants

JOHN RICH, *Moderator*
Professor and Chair of Health Management and Policy
Drexel University School of Public Health

6:00 p.m.   Adjourn

C

Committee Biographies

Alan I. Leshner, Ph.D. (*Chair*), is chief executive officer of the American Association for the Advancement of Science (AAAS) and executive publisher of the journal *Science*, a post he has held since December 2001. From 1994 to 2001, Dr. Leshner was director of the National Institute on Drug Abuse at the National Institutes of Health. Prior to that, Dr. Leshner was the deputy director and acting director of the National Institute of Mental Health (NIMH). He went to NIMH from the National Science Foundation, where he held a variety of senior positions, focusing on basic research in the biological, behavioral, and social sciences; science policy; and science education. Dr. Leshner is an elected fellow of AAAS, the National Academy of Public Administration, the American Academy of Arts and Sciences, and many other professional societies. He is a member of the Institute of Medicine of the National Academy of Sciences and served on its governing council. He was appointed to the National Science Board by President George W. Bush in 2004 and reappointed by President Obama in 2011. Dr. Leshner received an undergraduate degree in psychology from Franklin and Marshall College and M.S. and Ph.D. degrees in physiological psychology from Rutgers University. He has been awarded six honorary doctor of science degrees.

Louis Arcangeli, M.Ed., is currently a part-time instructor in the department of criminal justice at Georgia State University, a position he has held since 2003. Mr. Arcangeli is retired from the Atlanta Police Department (APD), where his 33 years of service included 5 years as a deputy chief of police and 7 years as an elected pension fund trustee. While with the department, Mr. Arcangeli served as the deputy chief of APD planning for the 1996 Olympic Games and the implementation of a new

E-911 Center and APD communications system. He has been a police instructor for the Georgia Public Safety Training Center and a Hunter Safety Instructor for the Georgia Department of Natural Resources, Wildlife Management Division. Mr. Arcangeli is a graduate of the Federal Bureau of Investigation National Academy and holds a master's degree in education from Georgia State University.

Alfred Blumstein, Ph.D., is university professor and J. Erik Jonsson Professor of Urban Systems and Operations Research in the H. John Heinz III College of Public Policy and Information Systems at Carnegie Mellon University. Before joining Heinz in 1969, Dr. Blumstein was at the Institute for Defense Analyses, where he was director of the Office of Urban Research and a member of the Research Council. He also served as the director of the Science and Technology Task Force for the President's Commission on Law Enforcement and Administration of Justice. Dr. Blumstein was a member of the National Academy of Sciences Committee on Research on Law Enforcement and the Administration of Justice from its founding in 1975 until 1986, serving as chairman from 1979 to 1984. He also served from 1979 to 1990 as chairman of the Pennsylvania Commission on Crime and Delinquency, the state's criminal justice planning agency, and as a member of the Pennsylvania Commission on Sentencing from 1986 to 1996. Dr. Blumstein's research during the past 20 years has covered many aspects of criminal justice phenomena and policy, including crime measurement, criminal careers, sentencing, deterrence and incapacitation, prison populations, flow through the system, demographic trends, juvenile violence, and drug-enforcement policy. Dr. Blumstein has also served as director of the National Consortium on Violence Research. He was appointed in 2012 as chair of the Science Advisory Board for the Office of Justice Programs in the U.S. Department of Justice. Dr. Blumstein was a 2007 recipient of the Stockholm Prize in Criminology. He is a member of the National Academy of Engineering. Dr. Blumstein received a bachelor's degree in engineering physics and a Ph.D. in operations research from Cornell University.

C. Hendricks Brown, Ph.D., is a professor of epidemiology and public health in the Miller School of Medicine at the University of Miami. He also holds adjunct professor positions in the departments of biostatistics and mental health at the Johns Hopkins Bloomberg School of Public Health. In addition, he is a senior research scholar at the American Institutes for Research and a collaborating senior scientist at the Oregon Center for Research to Practice. As director of the Prevention Science and Methodology Group, Dr. Brown leads a national network of 120 scientists and methodologists who are working on the design of preventive field trials and their analysis, particularly with advanced techniques for growth analysis and missing data. He is also the co-director of the multisite Center for Integrating Education and Prevention in Schools. Dr. Brown previously served as distinguished university health professor in the department of epidemiology and biostatistics in the College of Public Health at the University of South Florida. Recently, his work has focused on the prevention of serious mental disorders such as schizophrenia and the prevention of suicide. Funding from National Institute of Mental Health supports his research to evaluate the impact of antidepressants on suicide using multiple datasets. Dr. Brown has chaired or co-chaired a number of international meetings related to synthesizing the evidence of prevention studies and serves on numerous federal panels, advisory boards, and editorial boards. He completed his undergraduate work at Vanderbilt University and received an M.A. in chemistry and a Ph.D. in statistics from the University of Chicago.

Donald Carlucci, Ph.D., is the U.S. Army senior scientist for computational structural modeling at the U.S. Army Armament, Research, Development and Engineering Center, Picatinny Arsenal, where he has been employed since 1989. He was formerly chief of the Analysis and Evaluation Technology Division, Fuze and Precision Munitions Technology Directorate, responsible for the modeling and evaluation of cannon-launched munitions programs at Picatinny, and chief scientist for the XM982 Excalibur guided projectile. He also teaches graduate classes at Stevens Institute of Technology on Interior, Exterior and Terminal Ballistics as well as undergraduate classes on engineering design. Dr. Carlucci formerly held the position of development program officer (chief engineer) for Sense and Destroy Armor (SADARM). Prior to employment at Picatinny, he was a design engineer for Titanium Industries in Fairfield, New Jersey, and held positions as chief engineer, quality assurance manager, and purchasing manager for Hoyt Corporation, located in Englewood, New Jersey. He is a licensed professional engineer in the states of New Jersey and New York. He earned a doctorate in mechanical engineering and a master's degree in engineering (mechanical) from Stevens Institute of Technology and a bachelor of science degree in mechanical engineering from the New Jersey Institute of Technology.

BG (Ret.) Rhonda Cornum, M.D., Ph.D., is director of health strategy at TechWerks and a private consultant for resilience building within large organizations. She previously served as the first director of the U.S. Army's novel Comprehensive Soldier Fitness initiative. Before that, she served as assistant surgeon general for force projection. In this capacity, she was responsible for policies and procedures to prepare soldiers and units for deployment. She commanded the Landstuhl Regional Medical Center, which is the evacuation hub for Iraq, Afghanistan, Africa, and Europe, during the height of the Iraq and Afghanistan conflicts. Dr. Cornum sits on numerous committees and advisory boards, including the Advisory Committee on Former Prisoners of War for the Department of Veterans Affairs and the External Advisory Board for the Millennium Cohort Study. Dr. Cornum is board-certified in urology, a fellow of both the American College of Surgeons and the Aerospace Medical Association, a member of the American Society of Nutrition, and an adjunct professor at the Uniformed Services University of the Health Sciences. Her decorations include the Distinguished Service Medal, Legion of Merit, Distinguished Flying Cross, Bronze Star, Meritorious Service Medal (with four oak leaf clusters), Purple Heart, Air Medal, and Prisoner of War Medal. She received her Ph.D. in biochemistry and nutrition from Cornell University and an M.D. from the Uniformed Services University of the Health Sciences.

Paul K. Halverson, Dr.P.H., M.H.S.A., F.A.C.H.E., is the founding dean at the Indiana University Richard M. Fairbanks School of Public Health. He previously served as the director of health and state health officer of the Arkansas Department of Health and as the secretary of the Arkansas State Board of Health. He was a professor of public health and medicine at the University of Arkansas for Medical Sciences and an adjunct professor of public health at the University of North Carolina (UNC) at Chapel Hill. Dr. Halverson is also past president of the Association of State and Territorial Health Officials as well as past chair of the Public Health Accreditation Board. Prior to his move to Arkansas, Dr. Halverson served as a member of the Senior Biomedical Research Service at the Centers for Disease Control and Prevention (CDC). As the director of the Division of Public Health Systems Development and Research, Dr. Halverson had responsibility for strengthening the effectiveness of public health systems throughout the world. Prior to his appointment at CDC, Professor Halverson was a member of the faculty in the Department of Health Policy and Administration at the University of North Carolina School of Public Health. Prior to his appointment at UNC, Dr. Halverson served as a hospital administrator in Arizona, Minnesota, and Michigan. He earned a master's in health services administration from Arizona State University and a doctor of public health in health policy and administration from UNC at Chapel Hill.

Stephen W. Hargarten, M.D., M.P.H., is professor and chair of the department of emergency medicine, associate dean for the global health program, and director of the Injury Research Center at the Medical College of Wisconsin. He is also a member of the Injury Research Center's Education Core, which is focused on the development of a model injury prevention and control curriculum integrated across all 4 years of the medical student curriculum and the development of targeted injury prevention and control research training initiatives for medical and graduate students to prepare the next generation of injury research scientists. His research interests reflect an intersection of injury prevention and health policy to address the burden of injuries. Dr. Hargarten was the first chair of the statewide Committee on Trauma System Development for the Wisconsin State Health Department. He also served as chair of the Wisconsin Seat Belt Coalition and devoted considerable effort toward seat belt legislation in Wisconsin. He serves as a board member for Advocates of Highway and Auto Safety and the Association for Safe International Road Travel. He was the founding president of the Society for the Advancement of Violence and Injury Research. Dr. Hargarten received his M.D. from the Medical College of Wisconsin and an M.P.H. from the Johns Hopkins Bloomberg School of Public Health.

Ronald C. Kessler, Ph.D., is the McNeil Family Professor of Health Care Policy at Harvard Medical School, where he has served on the faculty since 1994. Prior to his most recent position, he was a professor of sociology and a program director at the University of Michigan's Institute for Social Research. Dr. Kessler is the principal investigator of the U.S. National Comorbidity Survey, the first nationally representative survey of the prevalence and correlates of mental disorders in the United States, and a co-director of the World Health Organization's World Mental Health Survey Initiative, a series of comparative community epidemiological surveys of the prevalence and correlates of mental disorders and treatment for those disorders in 28 countries around the world. He is also the principal investigator of the Harvard Medical School site for Army STARRS (Study To Assess Risk and Resilience in Servicemembers), a research program funded by the U.S. Army and the National Institute of Mental Health (NIMH) to study risk and protective factors for suicide among Army personnel. Dr. Kessler's research deals broadly with the social determinants of mental health and illness as studied from an epidemiological perspective. He is the author of more than 600 publications and the recipient of many awards for his research, including the Senior Scientist and MERIT awards from NIMH. He is a member of both the National Academy of Sciences and the Institute of Medicine. Dr. Kessler earned his Ph.D. in sociology from New York University and completed a postdoctoral fellowship in psychiatric epidemiology at the University of Wisconsin.

Gary Kleck, Ph.D., is the David J. Bordua Professor of Criminology and Criminal Justice and a courtesy professor of law at the Florida State University, where he has been on the faculty since 1978. Dr. Kleck's research interests are in gun control, deterrence, crime control, and the study of violence. He is the winner of the 1993 Michael J. Hindelang Award, bestowed by the American Society of Criminology, which named his book *Point Blank: Guns and Violence in America* "the most outstanding contribution to criminology." Dr. Kleck's subsequent work *Armed: New Perspectives on Gun Control* was featured in the *Choice: Current Reviews for Academic Librarians* 39th annual Outstanding Academic Title List, which recognizes books for "excellence in scholarship and presentation, the significance of their contribution to their field, and their value as an important treatment of their topic." Dr. Kleck is a member of the American Society of Criminology and the Academy of Criminal Justice Sciences. He earned his B.A., M.A., and Ph.D. in sociology from the University of Illinois at Urbana-Champaign.

John A. Rich, M.D., M.P.H., is professor and chair of health management and policy at the Drexel University School of Public Health. He is also the director of the Center for Nonviolence and Justice at Drexel. His work has focused on African American men in urban settings. In 2006, Dr. Rich was granted a MacArthur Fellowship for his work to design "new models of health care that stretch across the boundaries of public health, education, social service, and justice systems to engage young men in caring for themselves and their peers." Prior to arriving at Drexel University, Dr. Rich served as the medical director of the Boston Public Health Commission. As a primary care doctor at Boston Medical Center, he created the Young Men's Health Clinic and initiated the Boston

HealthCREW, a program to train inner-city young men to become peer health educators. He published a book about urban violence titled *Wrong Place, Wrong Time: Trauma and Violence in the Lives of Young Black Men* (Johns Hopkins University Press, 2009). In 2009, Dr. Rich was inducted into the Institute of Medicine of the National Academy of Sciences. He earned his A.B. degree in English from Dartmouth College, his M.D. from Duke University School of Medicine, and his M.P.H. from the Harvard School of Public Health.

Jeffrey W. Runge, M.D., is a principal at The Chertoff Group, a firm providing business risk management and security sector advisory services, and president of Biologue, Inc., a consulting firm specializing in biodefense, medical preparedness, and injury prevention and control. He is also an adjunct professor in the School of Medicine at the University of North Carolina at Chapel Hill. From 2005 to 2008, Dr. Runge served as the Department of Homeland Security's (DHS's) first chief medical officer and led the reorganization of biodefense operations into a new Office of Health Affairs (OHA). OHA acts as the principal adviser to all DHS component agencies on medical, biodefense, and workforce health issues. From 1984 to 2001, Dr. Runge practiced and taught emergency medicine in a North Carolina emergency department and trauma center and researched injury prevention, trauma care, and emergency service delivery. His leadership and innovation in road traffic safety brought him to Washington, DC, as the head of the National Highway Traffic Safety Administration, where he instituted programs that led to the first absolute declines in U.S. motor vehicle deaths in almost a decade and the lowest highway fatality rate in history. Dr. Runge is board-certified in emergency medicine and has published more than 60 articles in medical literature in the fields of emergency medicine, traffic injury control, and medical preparedness. Dr. Runge is a graduate of the University of the South in Sewanee, Tennessee, and received his medical degree from the Medical University of South Carolina.

Susan B. Sorenson, Ph.D., is professor of social policy and practice and professor of health and societies at the University of Pennsylvania. She is a senior fellow with the Center for Public Health Initiatives and the director of the Evelyn Jacobs Ortner Center on Family Violence. She previously taught and conducted research for 20 years at the University of California, Los Angeles (UCLA), School of Public Health. Dr. Sorenson has published widely on the epidemiology and prevention of violence, including the areas of homicide, suicide, sexual assault, child abuse, battering, and firearms. A primary focus of her work is the social context in which violence occurs, specifically, the norms that shape whether and how violence is tolerated. In addition to her academic work, Dr. Sorenson has served on the board of directors and advisory boards of local community-based organizations, state government agencies, and university injury prevention centers. In 1991, she co-founded the Violence Prevention Coalition of Greater Los Angeles. She was a consultant to President Clinton's National Advisory Council on Violence Against Women; a consultant to the United Nations Children's Fund May 2000 report *Domestic Violence Against Women and Girls*; and a member of the advisory panel for the 2001 U.S. Surgeon General's Report on Youth Violence. She is the author of a 2008 World Health Organization report on health indicators of violence against children in low- and middle-income countries. Dr. Sorenson earned a B.S. in sociology and psychology from the Iowa State University, an M.S. in psychology from the Illinois Institute of Technology, and a Ph.D. in clinical psychology from the University of Cincinnati. Dr. Sorenson completed a postdoctoral fellowship at the UCLA School of Public Health.

David Vlahov, Ph.D., R.N., FAAN, is dean and professor at the University of California, San Francisco, School of Nursing. He previously served as professor of epidemiology at Johns Hopkins University and Columbia University and held adjunct positions at the New York University (NYU) College of Nursing and at the medical schools of Cornell, Mount Sinai, and NYU. He also served as co-director of the Robert Wood Johnson Foundation's Health and Society Scholars program. Dr. Vlahov's research interests are in epidemiology, infectious diseases, substance abuse, and mental health. He has conducted studies of urban populations in Baltimore for more than 20 years and has led epidemiological studies in Harlem and the Bronx that have served as a platform for subsequent individual- and community-level intervention studies and community-based participatory research to address social determinants of health. Dr. Vlahov established the International Society for Urban Health, serving as its first president, and also served on the New York City Board of Health. He was a visiting professor at the Medical School in Belo Horizonte, Brazil, developing its programs in urban health, and an expert consultant to the World Health Organization's Urban Health Center in Kobe, Japan. Dr. Vlahov is the editor-in-chief of the *Journal of Urban Health*, has edited 3 books on urban health, and has published more than 610 scholarly papers. He received his baccalaureate in history from Earlham College, his bachelor's and master's degrees in nursing from the University of Maryland, and his doctorate in epidemiology from the Johns Hopkins Bloomberg School of Public Health.